IS LIFE WORTH LIVING?
BY
WILLIAM HURRELL MALLOCK

Is Life Worth Living? By William Hurrell Mallock

CHAPTER I.

THE NEW IMPORT OF THE QUESTION.

A change was coming over the world, the meaning and direction of which even still is hidden from us, a change from era to era.—Froude's History of England, ch. i.

What I am about to deal with in this book is a question which may well strike many, at first sight, as a question that has no serious meaning, or none at any rate for the sane and healthy mind. I am about to attempt inquiring, not sentimentally, but with all calmness and sobriety, into the true value of this human life of ours, as tried by those tests of reality which the modern world is accepting, and to ask dispassionately if it be really worth the living. The inquiry certainly has often been made before; but it has never been made properly; it has never been made in the true scientific spirit. It has always been vitiated either by diffidence or by personal feeling; and the positive school, though they rejoice to question everything else, have, at least in this country, left the worth of life alone. They may now and then, perhaps, have affected to examine it; but their examination has been merely formal, like that of a customs-house officer, who passes a portmanteau, which he has only opened. They have been as tender with it as Don Quixote was with his mended helmet, when he would not put his card-paper vizor to the test of the steel sword. I propose to supply this deficiency in their investigations. I propose to apply exact thought to the only great subject to which it has not been applied already.

To numbers, as I have just said, this will of course seem useless. They will think that the question never really was an open one; or that, if it ever were so, the common sense of mankind has long ago finally settled it. To ask it again, they will think idle, or worse than idle. It will express to them, if it expresses anything, no perplexity of the intellect, but merely some vague disease of the feelings. They will say that it is but the old ejaculation of satiety or despair, as old as human nature itself; it is a kind of maundering common to all moral dyspepsia; they have often heard it before, and they wish they may never hear it again.

But let them be a little less impatient. Let them look at the question closer, and more calmly; and it will not be long before its import begins to change for them. They will see that though it may have often been asked idly, it is yet capable of a meaning that is very far from idle; and that however old they may think it, yet as asked by our generation it is really completely new—that it bears a meaning which is indeed not far from any one of them, but which is practical and pressing—I might almost say portentous—and which is something literally unexampled in the past history of mankind.

I am aware that this position is not only not at first sight obvious, but that, even when better understood, it will probably be called false. My first care, therefore, will be to explain it at length, and clearly. For this purpose we must consider two points in order; first, what is the exact doubt we intend to express by our question; and next, why in our day this doubt should have such a special and fresh significance.

Let us then make it quite plain, at starting, that when we ask 'Is life worth living?' we are not asking whether its balance of pains is necessarily and always in excess of its balance of pleasures. We are not asking whether any one has been, or whether any one is happy. To the unjaundiced eye nothing is more clear than that happiness of various kinds has been, and is, continually attained by men. And ingenious pessimists do but waste their labour when they try to convince a happy man that he really must be miserable. What I am going to discuss is 4not the superfluous truism that life has been found worth living by many; but the profoundly different proposition that it ought to be found worth living by all. For this is what life is pronounced to be, when those claims are made for it that at present universally are made; when, as a general truth, it is said to be worth living; or when any of those august epithets are applied to it that are at present applied so constantly. At present, as we all know, it is called sacred, solemn, earnest, significant, and so forth. To withhold such epithets is considered a kind of blasphemy. And the meaning of all such language is this: it means that life has some deep inherent worth of its own, beyond what it can acquire or lose by the caprice of circumstance—a worth, which though it may be most fully revealed to a man, through certain forms of success, is yet not destroyed or made a minus quantity by failure. Certain forms of love, for instance, are held in a special way to reveal this worth to us; but the worth that a successful love is thus supposed to reveal is a worth that a hopeless love is supposed not to destroy. The worth is a part of life's essence, not a mere chance accident, as health or riches are; and we are supposed to lose it by no acts but our own.

Now it is evident that such a worth as this, is, in one sense, no mere fancy. Numbers actually have found it; and numbers actually still continue to find 5it. The question is not whether the worth exists, but on what is the worth based. How far is the treasure incorruptible; and how far will our increasing knowledge act as moth and rust to it? There are some things whose value is completely established by the mere fact that men do value them. They appeal to single tastes, they defy further analysis, and they thus form, as it were, the bases of all pleasures and happiness. But these are few in number; they are hardly ever met with in a perfectly pure state; and their effect, when they are so met, is either momentary, or far from vivid. As a rule they are found in combinations of great complexity, fused into an infinity of new substances by the action of beliefs and associations; and these two agents are often of more importance in the result than are the things they act upon. Take for instance a boy at Eton or Oxford, who affects a taste in wine. Give him a bottle of gooseberry champagne; tell him it is of the finest brand, and that it cost two hundred shillings a dozen. He will sniff, and wink at it in ecstasy; he will sip it slowly with an air of knowing reverence; and his enjoyment of it probably will be far keener, than it would be, were the wine really all he fancies it, and he had lived years enough to have come to discern its qualities. Here the part played by belief and associations is of course evident. The boy's enjoyment is real, and it rests to a certain ex6tent on a foundation of solid fact; the taste of the gooseberry champagne is an actual pleasure to his palate. Anything nauseous, black dose for instance, could never raise him to the state of delight in question. But this simple pleasure of sense is but a small part of the pleasure he actually experiences. That pleasure, as a whole, is a highly complex thing, and rests mainly on a basis that, by a little knowledge, could be annihilated in a moment. Tell the boy what the champagne really is, he has been praising; and the state of his mind and face will undergo a curious transformation. Our sense of the worth of life is similar in its complexity to the boy's sense of the worth of his wine. Beliefs and associations play exactly the same part in it. The beliefs in this last case may of course be truer. The question that I have to ask is, are they? In some individual cases certainly, they have not been. Miss Harriet Martineau, for instance, judging life from her own experience of it, was quite persuaded that it was a most solemn and satisfactory thing, and she has told the world as much, in no hesitating manner. But a part at least of the solemn satisfaction she felt in it was due to a grotesque over-estimate of her own social and intellectual importance. Here, then, was a worth in life, real enough to the person who found it, but which a little knowledge of the world would have at once taken away from her. Does the gen7eral reverence with which life is at present regarded rest in any degree upon any similar misconception? And if so, to what extent does it? Will it fall to pieces before the breath of a larger knowledge? or has it that firm foundation in fact that will enable it to survive in spite of all enlightenment, and perhaps even to increase in consequence of it?

Such is the outline of the question I propose to deal with. I will now show why it is so pressing, and why, in the present crisis of thought, it is so needful that it should be dealt with. The first impression it produces, as I have said, is that it is superfluous. Our belief in life seems to rest on too wide an experience for us to entertain any genuine doubt of the truth of it. But this first impression does not go for much. It is a mere superficial thing, and will wear off immediately. We have but to remember that a belief that was supposed to rest on an equally wide basis—the belief in God, and in a supernatural order—has in these days, not been questioned only, but has been to a great degree, successfully annihilated. The only philosophy that belongs to the present age, the only philosophy that is a really new agent in progress, has declared this belief to be a dissolving dream of the past. And this belief, as we shall see presently, is, amongst civilized men at least, far older than the belief in life; it has been far more widely spread, and experience has been held to confirm it with an equal certainty. If this then is inevitably disintegrated by the action of a widening knowledge, it cannot be taken for granted that the belief in life will not fare likewise. It may do so; but until we have examined it more closely we cannot be certain that it will. Common consent and experience, until they are analysed, are fallacious tests for the seekers after positive truth. The emotions may forbid us to ask our question; but in modern philosophy the emotions play no part as organs of discovery. They are facts in themselves, and as such are of course of value; but they point to no facts beyond themselves. That men loved God and felt his presence close to them proves nothing, to the positive thinker, as to God's existence. Nor will the mere emotion of reverence towards life necessarily go any farther towards proving that it deserves reverence. It is distinctly asserted by the modern school that the right state in which to approach everything is a state of enlightened scepticism. We are to consider everything doubtful, until it is proved certain, or unless, from its very nature, it is not possible to doubt it.

Nor is this all; for, apart from these modern canons, the question of life's worth has, as a matter of fact, been always recognised as in a certain sense an open one. The greatest intellects of the world, in all ages, have been at times inclined to doubt it. And these times have not seemed to them times of blindness; but on the contrary, of specially clear insight. Scales, as it were, have fallen from their eyes for a moment or two, and the beauty and worth of existence has appeared to them as but a deceiving show. An entire book of the Hebrew Scriptures is devoted to a deliberate exposition of this philosophy. In 'the most high and palmy state' of Athens it was expressed fitfully also as the deepest wisdom of her most triumphant dramatist.[1] And in Shakspeare it appears so constantly, that it must evidently have had for him some directly personal meaning.

This view, however, even by most of those who have held it, has been felt to be really only a half-view in the guise of a whole one. To Shakspeare, for instance, it was full of a profound terror. It crushed, and appalled, and touched him; and there was not only implied in it that for us life does mean little, but that by some possibility it might have meant much. Or else, if the pessimism has been more complete than this, it has probably been adopted as a kind of solemn affectation, or has else been lamented as a form of diseased melancholy. It is a view that healthy intellects have hitherto declined to entertain. Its advocates have been met with neglect, contempt, or castigation, not with arguments. They have been pitied as insane, avoided as cynical, or passed over as frivolous. And yet, but for one reason, to that whole European world whose progress we are now inheriting, this view would have seemed not only not untenable, but even obvious. The emptiness of the things of this life, the incompleteness of even its highest pleasures, and their utter powerlessness to make us really happy, has been, at least for fifteen hundred years, a commonplace, both with saints and sages. The conception that anything in this life could of itself be of any great moment to us, was considered as much a puerility unworthy of a man of the world, as a disloyalty to God. Experience of life, and meditation on life, seemed to teach nothing but the same lesson, seemed to preach a sermon de contemptu mundi. The view the eager monk began with, the sated monarch ended with. But matters did not end here. There was something more to come, by which this view was altogether transmuted, and which made the wilderness and the waste place at once blossom as the rose. Judged of by itself, this life would indeed be vanity; but it was not to be judged of by itself. All its ways seemed to break short aimlessly into precipices, or to be lost hopelessly in deserts. They led to no visible end. True; but they led to [11]ends that were invisible—to spiritual and eternal destinies, to triumphs beyond all hope, and portentous failures beyond all fear. This all men might see, if they would only choose to see. The most trivial of our daily actions became thus invested with an immeasurable meaning. Life was thus evidently not vanity, not an idiot's tale, not unprofitable; those who affected to think it was, were naturally disregarded as either insane or insincere: and we may thus admit that hitherto, for the progressive nations of the world, the worth of life has been capable of demonstration, and safe beyond the reach of any rational questioning.

But now, under the influence of positive thought, all this is changing. Life, as we have all of us inherited it, is coloured with the intense colours of Christianity; let us ourselves be personally Christians or not, we are instinct with feelings with regard to it that were applicable to it in its Christian state: and these feelings it is that we are still resolved to retain. As the most popular English exponent of the new school says: 'All positive methods of treating man, of a comprehensive kind, adopt to the full all that has ever been said about the dignity of man's moral and spiritual life.' But here comes the difficulty. This adoption we speak of must be justified upon quite new reasons. Indeed it is practically the boast of its advocates that it must be.[12] An extreme value, as we see, they are resolved to give to life; they will not tolerate those who deny its existence. But they are obliged to find it in the very place where hitherto it has been thought to be conspicuous by its absence. It is to be found in no better or wider future, where injustice shall be turned to justice, trouble into rest, and blindness into clear sight; for no such future awaits us. It is to be found in life itself, in this earthly life, this life between the cradle and the grave; and though imagination and sympathy may enlarge and extend this for the individual, yet the limits of its extension are very soon arrived at. It is limited by the time the human race can exist, by the space in the universe that the human race occupies, and the capacities of enjoyment that the human race possesses. Here, then, is a distinct and intelligible task that the positive thinkers have set themselves. They have taken everything away from life that to wise men hitherto has seemed to redeem it from vanity. They have to prove to us that they have not left it vain. They have to prove those things to be solid that have hitherto been thought hollow; those things to be serious that have hitherto been thought contemptible. They must prove to us that we shall be contented with what has never yet contented us, and that the widest minds will thrive within limits that have hitherto been thought too narrow for the narrowest.

Now, of course, so far as we can tell without examining the matter, they may be able to accomplish this revolution. There is nothing on the face of it that is impossible. It may be that our eyes are only blinded to the beauty of the earth by having gazed so long and so vainly into an empty heaven, and that when we have learnt to use them a little more to the purpose, we shall see close at hand in this life what we had been looking for, all this while, in another. But still, even if this revolution be possible, the fact remains that it is a revolution, and it cannot be accomplished without some effort. Our positive thinkers have a case to be proved. They must not beg the very point that is most open to contradiction, and which, when once duly apprehended, will be most sure to provoke it. If this life be not incapable of satisfying us, let them show us conclusively that it is not. But they can hardly expect that, without any such showing at all, the world will deliberately repel as a blasphemy what it has hitherto accepted as a commonplace.

This objection is itself so obvious that it has not escaped notice. But the very fact of its obviousness has tended to hide the true force of it, and coming so readily to the surface, it has been set down as superficial. It is, however, very constantly recognised, and is being met on all sides with a very elaborate answer. It is this answer that I shall now proceed to consider. It is a very important one, and it deserves our most close attention, as it contains the chief present argument for the positive faith in life. I shall show how this argument is vitiated by a fundamental fallacy.

It is admitted that to a hasty glance there may certainly seem some danger of our faith in life's value collapsing, together with our belief in God. It is admitted that this is not in the least irrational. But it is contended that a scientific study of the past will show us that these fears are groundless, and will reassure us as to the future. We are referred to a new branch of knowledge, the philosophy of history, and we are assured that by this all our doubts will be set at rest. This philosophy of history resembles, on an extended scale, the practical wisdom learnt by the man of the world. As long as a man is inexperienced and new to life, each calamity as it comes to him seems something unique and overwhelming, but as he lives on, suffers more of them, and yet finds that he is not overwhelmed, he learns to reduce them to their right dimensions, and is able, with sufficient self-possession, to let each of them teach some useful lesson to him.

Thus we, it is said, if we were not better instructed, might naturally take the present decline of faith to be an unprecedented calamity that was ushering in an eve of darkness and utter ruin. But the philosophy of history puts the whole matter in a different light. It teaches us that the condition of the world in our day, though not normal, is yet by no means peculiar. It points to numerous parallels in former ages, and treats the rise and fall of creeds as regular phenomena in human history, whose causes and recurrence we can distinctly trace. Other nations and races have had creeds, and have lost them; they have thought, as some of us think, that the loss would ruin them: and yet they have not been ruined. Creeds, it is contended, were imaginative, provisional, and mistaken expressions of the underlying and indestructible sense of the nobility of human life. They were artistic, not scientific. A statue of Apollo, for instance, or a picture of the Madonna, were really representations of what men aimed at producing on earth, not of what actually had any existence in heaven. And if we look back at the greatest civilisations of antiquity, we shall find, it is said, that what gave them vigour and intensity were purely human interests: and though religion may certainly have had some reflex action on life, this action was either merely political or was else injurious.

It is thus that intense Greek life is presented to us, the influence of which is still felt in the world. Its main stimulus we are told was frankly human. It would have lost none of its keenness if its theology had been taken from it. And there, it is said, we see 16the positive worth of life; we see already realised what we are now growing to realise once more. Christianity, with its supernatural aims and objects, is spoken of as an 'episode of disease and delirium;' it is a confusing dream, from which we are at last awaking; and the feelings of the modern school are expressed in the following sentence of a distinguished modern writer:2 'Just as the traveller,' he says, 'who has been worn to the bone by years of weary striving among men of another skin, suddenly gazes with doubting eyes upon the white face of a brother, so if we travel backwards in thought over the darker ages of the history of Europe we at length reach back with such bounding heart to men who had like hopes with ourselves, and shake hands across that vast with … our own spiritual ancestors.'

Nor are the Greeks the only nation whose history is supposed to be thus so reassuring to us. The early Jews are pointed to, in the same way, as having felt pre-eminently the dignity of this life, and having yet been absolutely without any belief in another. But the example, which for us is perhaps the most forcible of all, is to be found in the history of Rome, during her years of widest activity. We are told to look at such men as Cicero or as Cæsar—above all to 17such men as Cæsar—and to remember what a reality life was to them. Cæsar certainly had little religion enough; and what he may have had, played no part in making his life earnest. He took the world as he found it, as all healthy men have taken it; and, as it is said, all healthy men will still continue to take it. Nor was such a life as Cæsar's peculiar to himself. It represents that purely human life that flourished generally in such vigour amongst the Romans. And the consideration of it is said to be all the more instructive, because it flourished in the face of just the same conditions that we think so disheartening now. There was in those times, as there is in ours, a wide disintegration of the old faiths; and to many, then as now, this fact seemed at once sad and terrifying. As we read Juvenal, Petronius, Lucian, or Apuleius, we are astounded at the likeness of those times to these. Even in minute details, they correspond with a marvellous exactness. And hence there seems a strange force in the statement that history repeats itself, and that the wisdom learnt from the past can be applied to the present and the future.

But all this, though it is doubtless true, is in reality only half the truth; and as used in the arguments of the day, it amounts practically to a profound falsehood. History in a certain sense, of course, does repeat itself; and the thing that has been is in a certain sense the thing that shall be.18 But there is a deeper and a wider sense in which, this is not so. Let us take the life of an individual man, for instance. A man of fifty will retain very likely many of the tastes and tricks that were his, when a boy of ten: and people who have known him long will often exclaim that he is just the same as he always was. But in spite of this, they will know that he is very different. His hopes will have dwindled down; the glow, the colour, and the bright haze will have gone from them; things that once amused him will amuse him no more: things he once thought important, he will consider weary trifles; and if he thinks anything serious at all, they will not be things he thought serious when a boy. The same thing is true of the year, and its changing seasons. The history of a single year may be, in one sense, said to repeat itself every day. There is the same recurrence of light and darkness, of sunrise and of sunset: and a man who had lived only for a month or two, might fancy that this recurrence was complete. But let him live a little longer, and he will come to see that this is not so. Slowly through the summer he will begin to discern a change; until at last he can contrast the days and nights of winter with the days and nights of summer, and see how flowers that once opened fresh every morning, now never open or close at all. Then he will see that the two seasons, though in many 19points so like each other, are yet, in a far deeper way, different.

And so it is with the world's history. Isolate certain phenomena, and they do, without doubt, repeat themselves; but it is only when isolated that they can be said to do so. In many points the European thought and civilisation of to-day may seem to be a repetition of what has been before; we may fancy that we recognise our brothers in the past, and that we can, as the writer above quoted says, shake hands with them across the intervening years. But this is really only a deceiving fancy, when applied to such deep and universal questions as those we have now to deal with—to religion, to positive thought, and to the worth of life. The positivists and the unbelievers of the modern world, are not the same as those of the ancient world. Even when their language is identical, there is an immeasurable gulf between them. In our denials and assertions there are certain new factors, which at once make all such comparisons worthless. The importance of these will by-and-by appear more clearly, but I shall give a brief account of them now.

The first of these factors is the existence of Christianity, and that vast and undoubted change in the world of which it has been at once the cause and the index. It has done a work, and that work still remains: and we all feel the effects of it, whether we will or no. Described in the most general way, that work has been this. The supernatural, in the ancient world, was something vague and indefinite: and the classical theologies at any rate, though they were to some extent formal embodiments of it, could embody really but a very small part. Zeus and the Olympian hierarchies were dimly perceived to be encircled by some vaster mystery; which to the popular mind was altogether formless, and which even such men as Plato could only describe inadequately. The supernatural was like a dim and diffused light, brighter in some places, and darker in others, but focalised and concentrated nowhere. Christianity has focalised it, united into one the scattered points of brightness, and collected other rays that were before altogether imperceptible. That vague 'idea of the good,' of which Plato said most men dimly augured the existence, but could not express their augury, has been given a definite shape to by Christianity in the form of its Deity. That Deity, from an external point of view, may be said to have acquired His sovereignty as did the Roman Cæsar. He absorbed into His own person the offices of all the gods that were before him, as the Roman Cæsar absorbed all the offices of the state; and in His case also, as has been said of the Roman Cæsar, the whole was immeasurably greater than the mere sum of the parts. Scientifically and philosophically He became the first cause of the world; He became the father of the human soul, and its judge; and what is more, its rest and its delight, and its desire. Under the light of this conception, man appeared an ampler being. His thoughts were for ever being gazed on by the great controller of all things; he was made in the likeness of the Lord of lords; he was of kin to the power before which all the visible world trembled; and every detail in the life of a human soul became vaster, beyond all comparison, than the depths of space and time. But not only did the sense of man's dignity thus develop, and become definite. The accompanying sense of his degradation became intenser and more definite also. The gloom of a sense of sin is to be found in Æschylus, but this gloom was vague and formless. Christianity gave to it both depth and form; only the despair that might have been produced in this way was now softened by hope. Christianity has, in fact, declared clearly a supernatural of which men before were more or less ignorantly conscious. The declaration may or may not have been a complete one, but at any rate it is the completest that the world has yet known. And the practical result is this: when we, in these days, deny the supernatural, we are denying it in a way in which it was never denied before. Our denial is beyond all comparison more complete. The supernatural, for the ancient world, was like a perfume scenting life, out of a hundred different vessels, of which only two or three were visible to the same men or nations. They therefore might get rid of these, and yet the larger part of the scent would still remain to them. But for us, it is as though all the perfume had been collected into a single vessel; and if we get rid of this, we shall get rid of the scent altogether. Our air will be altogether odourless.

The materialism of Lucretius is a good instance of this. In many ways his denials bear a strong resemblance to ours. But the resemblance ceases a little below the surface. He denied the theology of his time as strongly as our positive thinkers deny the theology of ours. But the theology he denied was incomplete and puerile. He was not denying any 'All-embracer and All-sustainer,' for he knew of none such. And his denial of the gods he did deny left him room for the affirmation of others, whose existence, if considered accurately, was equally inconsistent with his own scientific premises. Again, in his denial of any immortality for man, what he denied is not the future that we are denying. The only future he knew of was one a belief in which had no influence on us, except for sadness. It was a protraction only of what is worst in life; it was in no way a completion of what is best in it. But with us the case is altogether different. Formerly the supernatural could not be denied completely, because it was not known completely. Not to affirm is a very different thing from to deny. And many beliefs which the positivists of the modern world are denying, the positivists of the ancient world more or less consciously lived by.

Next, there is this point to remember. Whilst during the Christian centuries, the devotion to a supernatural and extramundane aim has been engendering, as a recent writer has observed with indignation, a degrading 'pessimism as to the essential dignity of man,'[3] the world which we have been to a certain extent disregarding has been changing its character for us. In a number of ways, whilst we have not been perceiving it, its objective grandeur has been dwindling; and the imagination, when again called to the feat, cannot reinvest it with its old gorgeous colouring. Once the world, with the human race, who were the masters of it, was a thing of vast magnitude—the centre of the whole creation. The mind had no larger conceptions that were vivid enough to dwarf it. But now all this has changed. In the words of a well-known modern English historian, 'The floor of heaven, inlaid with stars, has sunk back into an infinite abyss of immeasurable space; and the firm earth itself, unfixed from its foundations, is seen to be but a small atom in the awful easiness of the universe.'[4] The whole position, indeed, is reversed. The skies once seemed to pay the earth homage, and to serve it with light and shelter. Now they do nothing, so far as the imagination is concerned, but spurn and dwarf it. And when we come to the details of the earth's surface itself, the case is just the same. It, in its extent, has grown little and paltry to us. The wonder and the mystery has gone from it. A Cockney excursionist goes round it in a holiday trip; there are no

Golden cities, ten months journey deep,
In far Tartarian wilds;[5]
nor do the confines of civilisation, melt as they once did, into any unknown and unexplored wonderlands. And thus a large mass of sentiment that was once powerful in the world is now rapidly dwindling, and, so far as we can see, there is nothing that can

ever exactly replace it. Patriotism, for instance, can never again be the religion it was to Athens, or the pride it was to Rome. Men are not awed and moved as once they were by local and material splendours. The pride of life, it is true, is still eagerly coveted; but by those at least who are most familiar with it, it is courted and sought for with a certain contempt and cynicism. It is treated like a courtesan, rather than like a goddess. Whilst as to the higher enthusiasm that was once excited by external things, the world in its present state could no more work itself up to this than a girl, after three seasons, could again go for dissipation to her dolls. She might look back to the time of dolls with regret. She might see that the interest they excited in her was, perhaps, far more pleasing than any she had found in love. But the dolls would never rival her lovers, none the less. And with man, and his aims and objects, the case is just the same. And we must remember that to realise keenly the potency of a past ideal, is no indication that practically it will ever again be powerful.

Briefly, then, the positive school of to-day we see thus far to be in this position. It has to make demands upon human life that were never made before; and human life is, in many ways, less able than it ever was to answer to them.

But this is not all. There is a third matter yet left to consider—a third factor in the case, peculiar to the present crisis. That is the intense self-consciousness that is now developed in the world, and which is something altogether new to it. During the last few generations man has been curiously changing. Much of his old spontaneity of action has gone from him. He has become a creature looking before and after; and his native hue of resolution has been sickled over by thought. We admit nothing now without question; we have learnt to take to pieces all motives to actions. We not only know more than we have done before, but we are perpetually chewing the cud of our knowledge. Thus positive thought reduces all religions to ideals created by man; and as such, not only admits that they have had vast influence, but teaches us also that we in the future must construct new ideals for ourselves. Only there will be this difference. We shall now know that they are ideals, we shall no longer mistake them for objective facts. But our positive thinkers forget this. They forget that the ideals that were once active in the world were active amongst people who thought that they were more than ideals, and who very certainly did mistake them for facts; and they forget how different their position will be, as soon as their true nature is recognised. There is no example, so far as I know, to be found in all history, of men having been stimulated or affected in any important way—none, at any rate, of their having been restrained or curbed—by a mere ideal that was known to have no reality to correspond to it. A child is frightened when its nurse tells it that a black man will come down the chimney and take it away. The black man, it is true, is only an ideal; and yet the child is affected. But it would cease to be affected the instant it knew this.

As we go on with our enquiry these considerations will become plainer to us. But enough has even now been said to show how distinct the present position is from any that have gone before it, and how little the experience of the past is really fitted to reassure us. Greek and Roman thought was positive, in our sense of the word, only in a very small degree. The thought of the other ancient empires was not positive at all. The oldest civilisation of which any record is left to us—the civilisation of Egypt—was based on a theism which, of all other theisms, most nearly approaches ours. And the doctrine of a future life was first learnt by the Jews from their masters during the Captivity. We search utterly in vain through history for any parallel to our own negations.

I have spoken hitherto of those peoples only whose history more or less directly has affected ours. But there is a vast portion of the human race with which, roughly speaking, our progress has had no connection; and the religions of these races, which are now for the first time beginning to be accurately studied, are constantly being appealed to in support of the positive doctrines. Thus it is urged by Mr. Leslie Stephen that 'the briefest outline of the religious history of mankind shows that 28 creeds which can count more adherents than Christianity, and have flourished through a longer period, have omitted all that makes the Christian doctrine of a future state 'valuable in the eyes of the supporters;' and Dr. Tyndall points with the same delighted confidence to the gospel of Buddhism, as one of 'pure human ethics, divorced not only from Brahma and the Brahminic Trinity, but even from the existence of God.'6 Many other such appeals are made to what are somewhat vaguely called 'the multitudinous creeds of the East;' but it is to Buddhism, in its various forms, that they would all seem to apply. Let us now consider the real result of them. Our positivists have appealed to Buddhism, and to Buddhism they shall certainly go. It is one of the vastest and most significant of all human facts. But its significance is somewhat different from what it is popularly supposed to be.

That the Buddhist religion has had a wide hold on the world is true. Indeed, forty per cent. of the whole human race at this moment profess it. Except the Judaic, it is the oldest of existing creeds; and beyond all comparison it numbers most adherents. And it is quite true also that it does not, in its pure state, base its teaching on the belief in any personal God, or offer as an end of action any happiness 29in any immortal life. But it does not for this reason bear any real resemblance to our modern Western positivism, nor give it any reason to be sanguine. On the contrary, it is most absolutely opposed to it; and its success is due to doctrines which Western positivism most emphatically repudiates. In the first place, so far from being based on exact thought, Buddhism takes for its very foundation four great mysteries, that are explicitly beyond the reach either of proof or reason; and of these the foremost and most intelligible is the transmigration and renewal of the existence of the individual. It is by this mystical doctrine, and by this alone, that Buddhism gains a hold on the common heart of man. This is the great fulcrum of its lever. Then further—and this is more important still—whereas the doctrine of Western positivism is that human life is good, or may be made good; and that in the possibility of the enjoyment of it consists the great stimulus to action; the doctrine of Buddhism is that human life is evil, and that man's right aim is not to gratify, but to extinguish, his desire for it. Love, for instance, as I have said before, is by most Western positivists held to be a high blessing. Buddhism tells us we should avoid it 'as though it were a pit of burning coals.' The most influential positive writer in England has said: 'I desire no future that will break the ties of the past.' Buddhism says that we should desire no present that will create any ties for the future. The beginning of the Buddhist teaching is the intense misery of life; the reward of Buddhist holiness is to, at last, live no longer. If we die in our sins, we shall be obliged to live again on the earth; and it will not be, perhaps, till after many lives that the necessity for fresh births will be exhausted. But when we have attained perfection, the evil spell is broken; and 'then the wise man,' it is said, 'is extinguished as this lamp.' The highest life was one of seclusion and asceticism. The founder of Buddhism was met, during his first preaching, with the objection that his system, if carried out fully, would be the ruin and the extermination of humanity. And he did not deny the charge; but said that what his questioners called ruin, was in reality the highest good.

It is then hard to conceive an appeal more singularly infelicitous than that which our modern positivists make to Buddhism. It is the appeal of optimists to inveterate pessimists, and of exact thinkers to inveterate mystics. If the consideration of it tells us anything of importance, it tells us this—that by far the largest mass of mankind that has ever been united by a single creed has explicitly denied every chief point that our Western teachers assert. So far then from helping to close the question we are to deal with—the question as to the positive worth of life, the testimony of Buddhism, if it be of any weight at all, can only go to convince us that the question is at once new and open—new, because it has never yet been asked so fully; and open, because in so far as it has been asked, nearly half mankind has repudiated the answer that we are so desirous of giving it. Mr. Leslie Stephen calls Buddhism 'a stupendous fact,' and I quite agree with him that it is so; but taken in connection with the present philosophy of Europe, it is hardly a fact to strengthen our confidence in the essential dignity of man, or the worth of man's life.

In short, the more we consider the matter, and the more various the points from which we do so, the more plain will it become to us that the problem the present age is confronted by is an altogether unanswered one; and that the closest seeming parallels to be found amongst other times and races, have far less really of parallelism in them than of contrast. The path of thought, as it were, has taken a sudden turn round a mountain; and our bewildered eyes are staring on an undreamed-of prospect. The leaders of progress thus far have greeted the sight with acclamation, and have confidently declared that we are looking on the promised land. But to the more thoughtful, and to the less impulsive, it is plain that a mist hangs over it, and that we have no right to be sure whether it is the promised land or no. They see grave reasons for making a closer scrutiny, and for asking if, when the mist lifts, what we see will be not splendour, but desolation.

Is Life Worth Living? By William Hurrell Mallock

CHAPTER II.

THE PRIZE OF LIFE.

'The kingdom of heaven is like unto a treasure hid in a field.'

Having thus seen broadly what is meant by that claim for life that we are about to analyse, we must now examine it more minutely, as made by the positive school themselves.

This will at once make evident one important point. The worth in question is closely bound up with what we call morality. In this respect our deniers of the supernatural claim to be on as firm a footing as the believers in it. They will not admit that the earnestness of life is lessened for them; or that they have opened any door either to levity or to licentiousness. It is true indeed that it is allowed occasionally that the loss of a faith in God, and of the life in a future, may, under certain circumstances, be a real loss to us. Others again contend that this loss is a gain. Such views as these, however, are not much to the purpose. For those even, according to whom life has lost most in this way, do not consider the loss a very important, still less a fatal one. The good is still to be an aim for us, and our devotion to it will be more valuable because it will be quite disinterested. Thus Dr. Tyndall informs us that though he has now rejected the religion of his earlier years, yet granting him proper health of body, there is 'no spiritual experience,' such as he then knew, 'no resolve of duty, no word of mercy, no act of self-renouncement, no solemnity of thought, no joy in the life and aspects of nature, that would not still be' his. The same is the implicit teaching of all George Eliot's novels; whilst Professor Huxley tells us that come what may to our 'intellectual beliefs and even education,' 'the beauty of holiness and the ugliness of sin' will remain for those that have eyes to see them, 'no mere metaphors, but real and intense feelings.' These are but a few examples, but the view of life they illustrate is so well known that these few will suffice. The point on which the modern positivist school is most vehement, is that it does not destroy, but that on the contrary it intensifies, the distinction between right and wrong.

And now let us consider what, according to all positive theories, this supremacy of morality means. It means that there is a certain course of active life, and a certain course only, by which life can be made by everyone a beautiful and a noble thing: and life is called earnest, because such a prize is within our reach, and solemn because there is a risk that we may fail to reach it. Were this not so, right and wrong could have no general and objective meaning. They would be purely personal matters—mere misleading names, in fact, for the private likes and the dislikes of each of us; and to talk of right, and good, and morality, as things that we ought all to conform to, and to live by, would be simply to talk nonsense. What the very existence of a moral system implies is, that whatever may be our personal inclinations naturally, there is some common pattern to which they should be all adjusted; the reason being that we shall so all become partakers in some common happiness, which is greater beyond comparison than every other kind.

Here we are presented with two obvious tasks: the first, to enquire what this happiness is, what are the qualities and attractions generally ascribed to it; the second, to analyse it, as it is thus held up to us, and to see if its professed ingredients are sufficient to make up the result.

To proceed then, all moral systems must, as we have just seen, postulate some end of action, an end to which morality is the only road. Further, this end is the one thing in life that is really worth attaining; and since we have to do with no life other than this one, it must be found amongst the days and years of which this short life is the aggregate. On the adequacy of this universal end depends the whole ques36tion of the positive worth of life, and the essential dignity of man.

That this is at least one way of stating the case has been often acknowledged by the positive moralists themselves. The following passage, for instance, is from the autobiography of J. S. Mill. 'From the winter of 1821,' he writes, 'when I first read Bentham.... I had what might truly be called an object in life, to be a reformer of the world.... I endeavoured to pick up as many flowers as I could by the way; but as a serious and permanent personal satisfaction to rest upon, my whole reliance was placed on this.... But the time came when I awakened from this as from a dream.... It occurred to me to put the question directly to myself: "Suppose that all your objects in life realised; that all the changes in institutions and opinions which you were looking forward to, could be completely effected in this very instant, would this be a very great joy and happiness to you?" And an irrepressible self-consciousness distinctly answered "No!" At this my heart sank within me: the whole foundation on which my life was constructed fell down.... The end had ceased to charm, and how could there ever again be any interest in the means? I seemed to have nothing left to live for.... The lines in Coleridge's "Dejection" exactly describe my case:—

37
"O grief without a pang, void, dark and drear,
A dreary, stifled, unimpassioned grief,
Which finds no natural outlet nor relief
In word, or sigh, or tear.
Work without hope draws nectar in a sieve,

And life without an object cannot live."'

And the foregoing confession is made more significant by the author's subsequent comment on it. 'Though my dejection,' he says, 'honestly looked at, could not be called other than egotistical, produced by the ruin, as I thought, of my fabric of happiness, yet the destiny of mankind was ever in my thoughts, and could not be separated from my own. I felt that the flaw in my life must be a flaw in life itself; and that the question was whether, if the reformers of society and government could succeed in their objects, and every person in the community were free, and in a state of physical comfort, the pleasures of life being no longer kept up by struggle and privation, would cease to be pleasures. And I felt that unless I could see some better hope than this for human happiness in general, my dejection must continue.' It is true that in Mill's case the dejection did not continue; and that in certain ways at which it is not yet time to touch, he succeeded, to his own satisfaction, in finding the end he was thus asking for. I only quote him to show how necessary he considered such an end to be. He acknowledged the fact, not only theoretically, or with his lips, but by months of misery, by intermittent thoughts of suicide, and by years of recurring melancholy. Some ultimate end of action, some kind of satisfying happiness—this, and this alone, he felt, could give any meaning to work, or make possible any kind of virtue. And a yet later authority has told us precisely the same thing. He has told us that the one great question that education is of value for answering, is this very question that was so earnestly asked by Mill. 'The ultimate end of education,' says Professor Huxley, 'is to promote morality and refinement, by teaching men to discipline themselves, and by leading them to see that the highest, as it is the only content, is to be attained not by grovelling in the rank and steaming valleys of sense, but by continually striving towards those high peaks, where, resting in eternal calm, reason discerns the undefined but bright ideal of the highest good—"a cloud by day, a pillar of fire by night."' And these words are an excellent specimen of the general moral exhortations of the new school.

Now all this is very well as far as it goes; and were there not one thing lacking, it would be just the answer that we are at present so anxious to elicit. But the one thing lacking, is enough to make it valueless. It may mean a great deal; but there is no possibility of saying exactly what it means. Before we can begin to strive towards the 'highest good,' we must know something of what this 'highest good' is. We must make this 'higher ideal' stand and unfold itself. If it cannot be made to do this, if it vanishes into mist as we near it, and takes a different shape to each of us as we recede from it; still more, if only some can see it, and to others it is quite invisible—then we must simply set it down as an illusion, and waste no more time in pursuit of it. But that it is not an illusion is the great positivist claim for it. Heaven and the love of God, we are told, were illusions. This 'highest good' we are offered, stands out in clear contradistinction to these. It is an actual attainable thing, a thing for flesh and blood creatures; it is to be won and enjoyed by them in their common daily life. It is, as its prophets distinctly and unanimously tell us, some form of happiness that results in this life to us, from certain conduct; it is a thing essentially for the present; and 'it is obviously,' says Professor Huxley, 'in no way affected by abbreviation or prolongation of our conscious life.'

This being the case, it is clearly not unreasonable to demand some explicit account of it; or if no sound account of it be extant, to enquire diligently what sort of account of it is possible. And let it be remembered that to make this demand is in no way to violate the great rule of Aristotle, and to demand a greater accuracy than the nature of the subject will admit of. The 'highest good,' it is quite possible, may be a vague thing; not capable, like a figure in Euclid, of being defined exactly. But many vague things can be described exactly enough for all practical purposes. They can be described so that we at once know what is meant, and so that we can at once find and recognise them. Feelings, characters, and personal appearance are things of this sort; so too is the taste of food, the style of furniture, or the general tone and tenour of our life, under various circumstances. And the 'good' we are now considering can surely be not less describable than these. When therefore our exact thinkers speak to us about the highest happiness, we want to know what meaning they attach to the words. Has Professor Huxley, for instance, ever enjoyed it himself, or does he ever hope to do so? If so, when, where, and how? What must be done to get it, and what must be left undone? And when it is got, what will it be like? Is it something brief, rapturous, and intermittent, as the language often used about it might seem to suggest to one? Is it known only in brief moments of Neoplatonic ecstasy, to which all the acts of life should be stepping stones? It certainly cannot be that. Our exact thinkers are essentially no mystics, and the highest happiness must be something far more solid than transcendental ecstasies. Surely, therefore, if it exists at all we must be able somewhere to lay our hands upon it. It is a pillar of fire by night; surely then it will be visible. It is to be lifted up, and is to draw all men unto it. It is nothing if not this: and we shall see more clearly if we consider the matter further.

This chief good, or this highest happiness, being the end of moral action, one point about it is at once evident. Its value is of course recognised by those who practise morality, or who enunciate moral systems. Virtuous men are virtuous because the end gained by virtue is an end that they desire to gain. But this is not enough; it is not enough that to men who are already seeking the good the good should appear in all its full attractiveness. It must be capable of being made attractive for those who do not know it, and who have never sought it, but who have, on the contrary, always turned away from everything that is supposed to lead to it. It must be able, in other words, not only to satisfy the virtuous of the wisdom of their virtue, it must be able to convince the vicious of the folly of their vice. Vice is only bad in the eye of the positive moralist because of the precious something that we are at the present moment losing by it. He can only convince us of our error by giving us some picture of our loss. And he must be able to do this, if his system is worth anything; and in promulgating his system he professes that he can do it. The physician's work is to heal the sick; his skill must not end in explaining his own health. It is clear that if a morality is incapable of being preached, it is useless to say that it is worthy of being practised. The statement will be meaningless, except to those for whom it is superfluous. It is therefore essential to the moral end that in some way or other it be generally presentable, so that its excellence shall appeal to some common sense in man. And again, be it observed, that we are demanding no mathematical accuracy. We demand only that the presentation shall be accurate enough to let us recognise its corresponding fact in life.

Now what is a code of morals, and why has the world any need of one? A code of morals is a number of restraining orders; it rigorously bids us walk in certain paths. But why? What is the use of bidding us? Because there are a number of other paths that we are naturally inclined to walk in. The right path is right because it leads to the highest kind of happiness; the wrong paths are wrong because they lead to lower kinds of happiness. But when men choose vice instead of virtue, what is happening? They are considering the lower or the lesser happiness better than the greater or the higher. It is this mistake that is the essence and cause of immorality; it is this mistake that mankind is ever inclined to make, and it is only because of this inclination that any moral system is of any general value.

Were we all naturally inclined to morality, the analysis of it, it is true, might have great speculative interest; but a moral system would not be needed as it is for a great practical purpose. The law, as we all know, has arisen because of transgressions, and the moralist has to meddle with human nature mainly because it is inconstant and corrupted. It is a wild horse that has not so much to be broken, once for all, as to be driven and reined in perpetually. And the art of the moralist is, by opening the mind's eye to the true end of life, to make us sharply conscious of what we lose by losing it. And the men to whom we shall chiefly want to present this end are not men, let us remember, who desire to see it, or who will seek for it of their own accord, but men who are turned away from it, and on whose sight it must be thrust. It is not the righteous but the sinners that have to be called to repentance. And not this only: not only must the end in question be thus presentable, but when presented it must be able to stand the inveterate criticism of those who fear being allured by it, who are content as they are, and have no wish to be made discontented. These men will submit it to every test by which they may hope to prove that its attractions are delusive. They will test it with reason, as we test a metal by an acid. They will ask what it is based upon, and of what it is compounded. They will submit it to an analysis as merciless as that by which their advisers have dissolved theism.

Here then is a fact that all positive morality presupposes. It presupposes that life by its very nature contains the possibility in it of some one kind of happiness, which is open to all men, and which is better than all others. It is sufficiently presentable even to those who have not experienced it; and its excellence is not vaguely apparent only, but can be exactly proved from obvious and acknowledged facts. Further, this happiness must be removed from its alternatives by some very great interval. The proudest, the serenest, the most successful life of vice, must be miserable when compared with the most painful life of virtue, and miserable in a very high degree; for morality is momentous exactly in proportion to the interval between the things to be gained and escaped by it. And unless this interval be a very profound one, the language at present current as to the importance of virtue, the dignity of life, and the earnestness of the moral struggle, will be altogether overstrained and ludicrous.

Now is such a happiness a reality or is it a myth? That is the great question. Can human life, cut off utterly from every hope beyond itself—can human life supply it? If it cannot, then evidently there can be no morality without religion. But perhaps it can. Perhaps life has greater capacities than we have hitherto given it credit for. Perhaps this happiness may be really close at hand for each of us, and we have only overlooked it hitherto because it was too directly before our eyes. At all events, wherever it is let it be pointed out to us. It is useless, as we have seen, if not generally presentable. To those who most need it, it is useless until presented. Indeed, until it is presented we are but acting on the maxim of its advocates by refusing to believe in its existence. 'No simplicity of mind,' says Professor Clifford, 'no obscurity of station, can escape the universal duty of questioning all that we believe.'

The question, then, that we want answered has by this time, I think, been stated with sufficient clearness, and its importance and its legitimacy been placed beyond a doubt. I shall now go on to explain in detail how completely unsatisfactory are the answers that are at present given it; how it is evaded by some and begged by others; and how those that are most plausible are really made worthless, by a subtle but profound defect.

These answers divide themselves into two classes, which, though invariably confused by those that give them, are in reality quite distinct and separable. Professor Huxley, one of the most vigorous of our positive thinkers, shall help us to understand these. He is going to tell us, let us remember, about the 'highest good'—the happiness, in other words, that we have just been discussing—the secret of our life's worth, and the test of all our conduct. This happiness he divides into two kinds.8 He says that there are two things that we may mean when we speak about it. We may mean the happiness of a society of men, or we may mean the happiness of the members of that society. And when we speak of morality, we may mean two things also; and these two things must be kept distinct. We may mean what Professor Huxley calls 'social morality,' and of this the test and object is the happiness of societies; or we may mean what he calls 'personal morality,' and of this the test and object is the happiness of individuals. And the answers which our positive moralists make to us divide themselves into two classes, according to the sort of happiness they refer to.

It is before all things important that this division be understood, and be kept quite clear in our minds, if we would see honestly what our positive modern systems amount to. For what makes them at present so very hard to deal with, is the fact that their exponents are perpetually perplexing themselves between these two classes of answers, first giving one, and then the other, and imagining that, by a kind of confusion of substance, they can both afford solutions of the same questions. Thus they continually speak of life as though its crowning achievement were some kind of personal happiness; and then being asked to explain the nature and basis of this, they at once shift their ground, and talk to us of the laws and conditions of social happiness. Professor Huxley will again supply us with a very excellent example. He starts with the thesis that both sorts of morality are strong enough to hold their own, without supernatural aid; and when we look to see on what ground he holds they are, we find it to consist in the following explanation that one is. 'Given,' he says, 'a society of human beings under certain circumstances, and the question whether a particular action on the part of one of its members will tend to increase the general happiness or not, is a question of natural knowledge, and as such is a perfectly legitimate subject of scientific inquiry.... If it can be shown by observation or experiment, that theft, murder, and adultery do not tend to diminish the happiness of society, then, in the absence of any but natural knowledge, they are not social immoralities.'

Now, in the above passage we have at least one thing. We have a short epitome of one of those classes of answers that our positive moralists are offering us. It is with this class that I shall deal in the following chapter; and point out as briefly as may be its complete irrelevance. After that, I shall go on to the other.

Is Life Worth Living? By William Hurrell Mallock

CHAPTER III.

SOCIOLOGY AS THE FOUNDATION OF MORALITY.

Society, says Professor Clifford, is the highest of all organisms;9 and its organic nature, he tells us, is one of those great facts which our own generation has been the first to state rationally. It is our understanding of this that enables us to supply morals with a positive basis. It is, he proceeds, because society is organic, 'that actions which, as individual, are insignificant, are massed together into ... important movements. Co-operation or band-work is the life of it.' And 'it is the practice of band-work,' he adds, that, unknown till lately though its nature was to us, has so moulded man as 'to create in him two specially human faculties, the conscience and the intellect;' of which the former, we are told, gives us the desire for the good, and the latter instructs us how to attain this desire by action. So too Professor Huxley, once more to recur to him, says that that state of man would be 'a true civitas Dei, in which each man's moral faculty shall be such as leads him to control all those desires which run counter to the good of mankind.' And J. S. 50Mill, whose doubts as to the value of life we have already dwelt upon, professed to have at last satisfied himself by a precisely similar answer. He had never 'wavered in the conviction,' he tells us, even all through his perplexity, that, if life had any value at all, 'happiness' was its one 'end,' and the 'test of its rule of conduct;' but he now thought that this end was to be attained by not making it the direct end, but 'by fixing the mind on some object other than one's own happiness; on the happiness of others—on the improvement of mankind.' The same thing is being told us on all sides, and in countless ways. The common name for this theory is Utilitarianism; and its great boast, and its special professed strength, is that it gives morals a positive basis in the acknowledged science of sociology. Whether sociology can really supply such a basis is what we now have to enquire. There are many practical rules for which it no doubt can do so; but will these rules correspond with what we mean by morals?

Now the province of the sociologist, within certain limits, is clear enough. His study is to the social body what the study of the physician is to the individual body. It is the study of human action as productive, or non-productive, of some certain general good. But here comes the point at issue—What is this general good, and what is included by it?51 The positive school contend that it is general happiness; and there, they say, is the answer to the great question—What is the test of conduct, and the true end of life? But though, as we shall see in another moment, there is some plausibility in this, there is really nothing in it of the special answer we want. Our question is, What is the true happiness? And what is the answer thus far?—That the true happiness is general happiness; that it is the happiness of men in societies; that it is happiness equally distributed. But this avails us nothing. The coveted happiness is still a locked casket. We know nothing as yet of its contents. A happy society neither does nor can mean anything but a number of happy individuals, so organised that their individual happiness is secured to them. But what do the individuals want? Before we can try to secure it for them, we must know that. Granted that we know what will make the individuals happy, then we shall know what will make society happy. And then social morality will be, as Professor Huxley says, a perfectly legitimate subject of scientific enquiry—then, but not till then. But this is what the positive school are perpetually losing sight of; and the reason of the confusion is not far to seek.

Within certain limits, it is quite true, the general good is a sufficiently obvious matter, and beyond the reach of any rational dispute. There are, therefore, certain rules with regard to conduct that we can arrive at and justify by strictly scientific methods. We can demonstrate that there are certain actions which we must never tolerate, and which we must join together, as best we may, to suppress. Actions, for instance, that would tend to generate pestilence, or to destroy our good faith in our fellows, or to render our lives and property insecure, are actions the badness of which can be scientifically verified.

But the general good by which these actions are tested is something quite distinct from happiness, though it undoubtedly has a close connection with it. It is no kind of happiness, high or low, in particular; it is simply those negative conditions required equally by every kind. If we are to be happy in any way, no matter what, we must of course have our lives, and, next to our lives, our health and our possessions secured to us. But to secure us these does not secure us happiness. It simply leaves us free to secure it, if we can, for ourselves. Once let us have some common agreement as to what this happiness is, we may then be able to formulate other rules for attaining it. But in the absence of any such agreement, the only possible aim of social morality, the only possible meaning of the general good, is not any kind or any kinds of happiness, but the security of those conditions without which all happiness would be impossible.

Suppose the human race were a set of canaries in a cage, and that we were in grave doubt as to what seed to give them—hemp-seed, rape-seed, or canary-seed, or all three mixed in certain proportions. That would exactly represent the state of our case thus far. There is the question that we want the positive school to answer. It is surely evident that, in this perplexity, it is beside the point to tell us that the birds must not peck each other's eyes out, and that they must all have access to the trough that we are ignorant how to fill.

The fault then, so continually committed by the positive school, is this. They confuse the negative conditions of happiness with the positive materials of it. Professor Huxley, in a passage I have already quoted, is caught, so to speak, in the very act of committing it. 'Theft, murder, and adultery,' all these three, it will be remembered, he classes together, and seems to think that they stand upon the same footing. But from what has just been pointed out, it is plain that they do not do so. We condemn theft and murder for one reason. We condemn adultery for quite another. We condemn the former because they are incompatible with any form of happiness. We condemn the latter because it is the supposed destruction of one particular form; or the substitution, rather, of a form supposed to be less complete, for another form supposed to be more complete. If the 'highest good,' if the best kind of happiness, be the end we are in search of, the truths of sociology will help us but a very short way towards it. By the practice of 'band-work' alone we shall never learn to construct a 'true Civitas Dei.' Band-work with the same perfection may be practised for opposite ends. Send an army in a just war or an unjust one, in either case it will need the same discipline. There must be order amongst thieves, as well as amongst honest men. There can be an orderly brothel as well as an orderly nunnery, and all order rests on co-operation. We presume co-operation. We require an end for which to co-operate.

I have already compared the science of sociology to that of medicine; and the comparison will again be a very instructive one. The aim of both sciences is to produce health; and the relation of health to happiness is in both cases the same. It is an important condition of the full enjoyment of anything: but it will by no means of itself give or guide us to the best thing. A man may be in excellent health, and yet, if he be prudent, be leading a degrading life. So, too, may a society. The Cities of the Plain may, for all we know to the contrary, have been in excellent social health; indeed, there is every reason to believe they were. They were, apparently, to a high degree strong and prosperous; and the sort of happiness that their citizens set most store by was only too generally attainable. There were not ten men to be found in them by whom the highest good had not been realised.

There are, however, two suppositions, on which the general good, or the health of the social organism, can be given a more definite meaning, and made in some sense an adequate test of conduct. And one or other of these suppositions is apparently always lurking in the positivist mind. But though, when unexpressed, and only barely assented to, they may seem to be true, their entire falsehood will appear the moment they are distinctly stated.

One of these suppositions is, that for human happiness health is alone requisite—health in the social organism including sufficient wealth and freedom; and that man's life, whenever it is not interfered with, will be moral, dignified, and delightful naturally, no matter how he lives it. But this supposition, from a moralist, is of course nonsense. For, were it true, as we have just seen, Sodom might have been as moral as the tents of

Abraham; and in a perfect state there would be a fitting place for both. The social organism indeed, in its highest state of perfection, would manifest the richest variety in the development of such various parts. It might consist of a number of motley communes of monogamists and of free-lovers, of ascetics and sybarites, of saints and παιδερασται—each of them being stones in this true Civitas Dei, this holy city of God. Of course it may be contended that this state of things would be desirable; that, however, is quite a different question. But whatever else it was, it would certainly not be moral, in any sense in which the word has yet been used.

The second supposition I spoke of, though less openly absurd than this one, is really quite as false. It consists of a vague idea that, for some reason or other, happiness can never be distributed in an equal measure to all, unless it be not only equal in degree but also the same in kind; and that the one kind that can be thus distributed is a kind that is in harmony with our conceptions of moral excellence. Now this is indeed so far true, that there are doubtless certain kinds of happiness which, if enjoyed at all, can be enjoyed by the few alone; and that the conditions under which alone the few can enjoy them disturb the conditions of all happiness for the many. The general good, therefore, gives us at once a test by which such kinds of happiness can be condemned. But to eliminate these will by no means leave us a residue of virtue; for these so far from being co-extensive with moral evil, do in reality lie only on the borders of it; and the condemnation attached to them is a legal rather than a moral one. It is based, that is, not so much on the kind of happiness itself as on the circumstances under which we are at present obliged to seek it. Thus the practice of seduction may be said to be condemned sufficiently by the misery brought by it to its victims, and its victims' families. But suppose the victims are willing, and the families complacent, this ground of condemnation goes; though in the eye of the moralist, matters in this last will be far worse than in the former. It is therefore quite a mistake to say that the kind of happiness which it is the end of life to realise is defined or narrowed down appreciably by the fact that it is a general end. Vice can be enjoyed in common, just as well as virtue; nor if wisely regulated will it exhaust the tastes that it appeals to. Regulated with equal skill, and with equal far-sightedness, it will take its place side by side with virtue; nor will sociology or social morality give us any reason for preferring the one to the other.

We may observe accordingly, that if happiness of some certain kind be the moral test, what Professor Huxley calls 'social morality'—the rule that is, for producing the negative conditions of happiness, it is not in itself morality at all. It may indeed become so, when the consciousness that we are conforming to it becomes one of the factors of our own personal happiness. It then suffers a kind of apotheosis. It is taken up into ourselves, and becomes part and parcel of our own personal morality. But it then becomes quite a different matter, as we shall see very shortly; and even then it supplies us with but a very small part of the answer.

Thus far what has been made plain is this. General, or social happiness, unless explained farther, is simply for moral purposes an unmeaning phrase. It evades the whole question we are asking; for happiness is no more differentiated by saying that it is general, than food is by saying that everyone at a table is eating it; or than a language is by saying that every one in a room is talking it. The social happiness of all of us means nothing but the personal happiness of each of us; and if social happiness have any single meaning—in other words, if it be a test of morals—it must postulate a personal happiness of some hitherto unexplained kind. Else sociology will be subsidiary to nothing but individual license; general law will be but the protection of individual lawlessness; and the completest social morality but the condition of the completest personal un-morality. The social organism we may compare to a yew-tree. Science will explain to us how it has grown up from the ground, and how all its twigs must have fitting room to expand in. It will not show us how to clip the yew-tree into a peacock. Morality, it is true, must rest ultimately on the proved facts of sociology; and this is not only true but evident. But it rests upon them as a statue rests upon its pedestal, and the same pedestal will support an Athenè or a Priapus.

The matter, however, is not yet altogether disposed of. The type of personal happiness that social morality postulates, as a whole, we have still to seek for. But a part of it, as I just pointed out, will, beyond doubt, be a willing obedience by each to the rules that make it in its entirety within the reach of all. About this obedience, however, there is a certain thing to remember: it must be willing, not enforced. The laws will of course do all they can to enforce it; but not only can they never do this completely, but even if they could, they would not produce morality. Conduct which, if willing, we should call highly moral, we shall, if enforced only, call nothing more than legal. We do not call a wild bear tame because it is so well caged that there is no fear of its attacking us; nor do we call a man good because, though his desires are evil, we have made him afraid to gratify them. Further, it is not enough that the obedience in question be willing in the sense that it does not give us pain. If it is to be a moral quality, it must also give us positive pleasure. Indeed, it must not so much be obedience to the law as an impassioned co-operation with it.

Now this, if producible, even though no further moral aim was connected with it, would undoubtedly be of itself a moral element. Suppose two pigs, for instance, had only a single wallowing-place, and each would like naturally to wallow in it for ever. If each pig in turn were to rejoice to make room for his brother, and were consciously to regulate his delight in becoming filthy himself by an equal delight in seeing his brother becoming filthy also, we should doubtless here be in the presence of a certain moral element. And though this, in a human society, might not carry us so far as we require to be carried, it would, without doubt, if producible, carry us a certain way. The question is, Is this moral element, this impassioned and unselfish co-operation with the social law, producible, in the absence of any farther end to which the social law is to be subordinate? The positive school apparently think it is; and this opinion has a seeming foundation in fact. We will therefore carefully examine what this foundation is, and see how far it is really able to support the weight that is laid upon it.

That fact, in itself a quite undoubted one, is the possession by man of a certain special and important feeling, which, viewed from its passive side, we call sympathy, and from its active side, benevolence. It exists in various degrees in different people, but to some degree or other it probably exists in all. Most people, for instance, if they hear an amusing story, at once itch to tell it to an appreciative friend; for they find that the amusement, if shared, is doubled. Two epicures together, for the same reason, will enjoy a dinner better than if they each dined singly. In such cases the enjoyment of another plays the part of a reflector, which throws one's own enjoyment back on one. Nor is this all. It is not only true that we often desire others to be pleased with us; we often desire others to be pleased instead of us. For instance, if there be but one easy chair in a room, one man will often give it up to another, and prefer himself to stand, or perhaps sit on the table. To contemplate discomfort is often more annoying than to suffer it.

This is the fact in human nature on which the positive school rely for their practical motive power. It is this sympathy and benevolence that is the secret of the social union; and it is by these that the rules of social morality are to be absorbed and attracted into ourselves, and made the directors of all our other impulses.

The feelings, however, that are thus relied on will be found, on consideration, to be altogether inadequate. They are undoubted facts, it is true, and are ours by the very constitution of our nature; but they do not possess the importance that is assigned to them, and their limits are soon reached. They are unequal in their distribution; they are partial and capricious in their action; and they are disturbed and counterbalanced by the opposite impulse of selfishness, which is just as much a part of our nature, and which is just as generally distributed. It must be a very one-sided view of the case that will lead us to deny this; and by such eclectic methods of observation we can support any theory we please. Thus there are many stories of unselfish heroism displayed by rough men on occasions such as shipwrecks, and displayed quite spontaneously. And did we confine our attention to this single set of examples, we might naturally conclude that we had here the real nature of man bursting forth in all its intense entirety—a constant but suppressed force, which we shall learn by-and-by to utilise generally. But if we extend our observations a little farther, we shall find another set of examples, in which selfishness is just as predominant as unselfishness was in the first set. The sailor, for instance, who might struggle to save a woman on a sinking ship, will trample her to death to escape from a burning theatre. And if we will but honestly estimate the composite nature of man, we shall find that the sailor, in this latter case, embodies a tendency far commoner, and far more to be counted on, than he does in the former. No fair student of life or history will, I think, be able to deny this. The lives of the world's greatest men, be they Goethes or Napoleons, will be the first to show us that it is so. Whilst the world's best men, who have been most successful in conquering their selfish nature, will be the first to bear witness to the persistent strength of it.

But even giving these unpromising facts the least weight possible, the case will practically be not much mended. The unselfish impulses, let them be diffused never so widely, will be found, as a general rule, to be very limited in power; and to be intense only for short periods, and under exceptional circumstances. They are intense only—in the absence of any further motive—when the thing to be won for another becomes invested for the moment with an abnormal value, and the thing to be lost by oneself becomes abnormally depreciated; when all intermediate possibilities are suddenly swept away from us, and the only surviving alternatives are shame and heroism. But this never happens, except in the case of great catastrophes, of such, for instance, as a shipwreck; and thus the only conditions under which an impassioned unselfishness can be counted on, are amongst the first conditions that we trust to progress to eliminate. The common state of life, then, when the feelings are in this normal state of tension, is all that in this connection we can really be concerned in dealing with. And there, unselfishness, though as sure a fact as selfishness, is, spontaneously and apart from a further motive, essentially unequal to the work it is asked to do. Thus, though as I observed just now, a man may often prefer to sit on a table and give up the arm-chair to a friend, there are other times when he will be very loth to do so. He will do so when the pleasure of looking at comfort is greater than the pleasure of feeling it. And in certain states of mind and body this is very often the case. But let him be sleepy and really in need of rest, the selfish impulse will at once eclipse the unselfish, and, unless under the action of some alien motive, he will keep the arm-chair for himself. So, too, in the case of the two epicures, if there be sufficient of the best dainties for both, each will feel that it is so much the better. But whenever the dainties in question cannot be divided, it will be the tendency of each to take them furtively for himself.

And when we come to the conditions of happiness the matter will be just the same. If without incommoding ourselves we can, as Professor Huxley says, repress 'all those desires which run counter to the good of mankind,' we shall no doubt all willingly do so; only in that case little more need be said. The 'Civitas Dei' we are promised may be left to take care of itself, and it will doubtless very soon begin 'to rise like an exhalation.' But if this self-repression be a matter of great difficulty, and one requiring a constant struggle on our part, it will be needful for us to intensely realise, when we abstain from any action, that the happiness it would take from others will be far greater than the happiness it would give to ourselves. Suppose, for instance, a man were in love with his friend's wife, and had engaged on a certain night to take her to the theatre. He would instantly give the engagement up could he know that the people in the gallery would be burnt to death if he did not. He would certainly not give it up because by the sight of his proceedings the moral tone of the stalls might be infinitesimally lowered; still less would he do so because another wife's husband might be made infinitely jealous. Whenever we give up any source of personal happiness for the sake of the happiness of the community at large, the two kinds of happiness have to be weighed together in a balance. But the latter, except in very few cases, is at a great disadvantage: only a part of it, so to speak, can be got into the scale. What adds to my sense of pleasure in the proportion of a million pounds may be only taxing society in the proportion of half a farthing a head. Unselfishness with regard to society is thus essentially a different thing from unselfishness with regard to an individual. In the latter case the things to be weighed together are commensurate: not so is the former. In the latter case, as we have seen, an impassioned self-devotion may be at times produced by the sudden presentation to a man of two extreme alternatives; but in the former case such alternatives are not presentable. I may know that a certain line of conduct will on the one hand give me great pleasure, and that on the other hand, if it were practised by everyone, it would produce much general mischief; but I shall know that my practising it, will, as a fact, be hardly felt at all by the community, or at all events only in a very small degree. And therefore my choice is not that of the sailor's in the shipwreck. It does not lie between saving my life at the expense of a woman's, or saving a woman's life at the expense of mine. It lies rather, as it were, between letting her lose her ear-ring and breaking my own arm.

It will appear, therefore, that the general conditions of an entirely undefined happiness form an ideal utterly unfitted to counterbalance individual temptation or, to give even willingness, let alone ardour, to the self-denials that are required of us. In the first place the conditions are so vague that even in the extremest cases the individual will find it difficult to realise that he is appreciably disturbing them. And in the second place, until he knows that the happiness in question is something of extreme value he will be unable to feel much ardour in helping to make it possible. If we knew that the social organism in its state of completest health had no higher pleasure than sleep and eating, the cause of its completest health would hardly excite enthusiasm. And even if we did not rebel against any sacrifices for so poor a result as this, we should at the best be resigned rather than blest in making them. The nearest approach to a moral end that the science of sociology will of itself supply to us is an end that, in all probability, men will not follow at all, or that will produce in them, if they do, no happier state than a passionless and passive acquiescence. If we want anything more than this we must deal with happiness itself, not with the negative conditions of it. We must discern the highest good that is within the reach of each of us, and this may perhaps supply us with a motive for endeavouring to secure the same blessing for all. But the matter depends entirely on what this highest good is—on the end to which, given the social health, the social health will be directed.

The real answer to this question can be given, as I have said before, in terms of the individual only. Social happiness is a mere set of ciphers till the unit of personal happiness is placed before it. A man's happiness may of course depend on other beings, but still it is none the less contained in himself. If our greatest delight were to see each other dance the can-can, then it might be morality for us all to dance. None the less would this be a happy world, not because we were all dancing, but because we each enjoyed the sight of such a spectacle. Many young officers take intense pride in their regiments, and the character of such regiments may in a certain sense be called a corporate thing. But it depends entirely on the personal character of their members, and all that the phrase really indicates is that a set of men take pleasure in similar things. Thus it is the boast of one young officer that the members of his regiment all spend too much, of another that they all drink too much, of another that they are distinguished for their high rank, and of another that they are distinguished for the lowness of their sensuality. What differentiates one regiment from another is first and before all things some personal source of happiness common to all its members.

And as it is with the character of a regiment, so too is it with the character of life in general. When we say that Humanity may become a glorious thing as a whole, we must mean that each man may attain some positive glory as an individual. What shall I get? and I? and I? and I? What do you offer me? and me? and me? This is the first question that the common sense of mankind asks. 'You must promise something to each of us,' it says, 'or very certainly you will be able to promise nothing to all of us.' There is no real escape in saying that we must all work for one another, and that our happiness is to be found in that. The question merely confronts us with two other facets of itself. What sort of happiness shall I secure for others? and what sort of happiness will others secure for me? What will it be like? Will it be worth having? In the positivist Utopia, we are told, each man's happiness is bound up in the happiness of all the rest, and is thus infinitely intensified. All mankind are made a mighty whole, by the fusing power of benevolence. Benevolence, however, means simply the wishing that our neighbours were happy, the helping to make them so, and lastly the being glad that they are so. But happiness must plainly be something besides benevolence; else, if I know that a man's highest happiness is in knowing that others are happy, all I shall try to procure for others is the knowledge that I am happy; and thus the Utopian happiness would be expressed completely in the somewhat homely formula, 'I am so glad that you are glad that I am glad.' But this is, of course, not enough. All this gladness must be about something besides itself. Our good wishes for our neighbours must have some farther content than that they shall wish us well in return. What I wish them and what they wish me must be something that both they and I, each of us, take delight in for ourselves. It will certainly be no delight to men to procure for others what they will take no delight in themselves, if procured by others for them. 'For a joyful life, that is to say a pleasant life,' as Sir Thomas More pithily puts it, 'is either evil; and if so, then thou shouldest not only help no man thereto, but rather as much as in thee lieth withdraw all men from it as noisome and hurtful; or else if thou not only mayest, but also of duty art bound to procure it for others, why not chiefly for thyself, to whom thou art bound to show as much favour and gentleness as to others?' The fundamental question is, then, what life should a man try to procure for himself? How shall he make it most joyful? and how joyful will it be when he has done his utmost for it? It is in terms of the individual, and of the individual only, that the value of life can at first be intelligibly stated. If the coin be not itself genuine, we shall never be able to make it so by merely shuffling it about from hand to hand, nor even by indefinitely multiplying it. A million sham bank notes will not make us any richer than a single one. Granting that the riches are really genuine, then the knowledge of their diffusion may magnify for each of us our own pleasure in possessing them. But it will only do this if the share that is possessed by each be itself something very great to begin with. Certain intense kinds of happiness may perhaps be raised to ecstasy by the thought that another shares them. But if the feeling in question be nothing more than cheerfulness, a man will not be made ecstatic by the knowledge that any number of other people are cheerful as well as he. When the happiness of two or more people rises to a certain temperature, then it is true a certain fusion may take place, and there may perhaps be a certain joint result, arising from the sum of the parts. But below this melting point no fusion or union takes place at all, nor will any number of lesser happinesses melt and be massed together into one great one. Two great wits may increase each other's brilliancy, but two half-wits will not make a single whole one. A bad picture will not become good by being magnified, nor will a merely readable novel become more than readable by the publication of a million copies of it. Suppose it were a matter of life and death to ten men to walk to York from London in a day. Were this feat a possible one, they might no doubt each do their best to help the others to accomplish it. But if it were beyond the power of each singly, they would not accomplish it as a body, by the whole ten leaving Charing Cross together, and each of them walking one tenth of the way. The distance they could all walk would be no greater than the distance they could each walk. In the same way the value of human life, as a whole, depends on the capacities of the individual human being, as an enjoying animal. If these capacities be great, we shall be eager in our desire to gratify them—certainly for ourselves, and perhaps also for others; and this second desire may perhaps be great enough to modify and to guide the first. But unless these capacities be great, and the means of gratifying them definite, our impulses on our own behalf will become weak and sluggish, whilst those on behalf of others will become less able to control them.

It will be apparent farther from this, that just as happiness, unless some distinct positive quality, gains nothing as an end of action, either in value or distinctness, by a mere diffusion in the present—by an extension, as it were, laterally—so will it gain nothing further by giving it another dimension, and by prospectively increasing it in the future. We must know what it is first, before we know whether it is capable of increase. Apart from this knowledge, the conception of progress and the hope of some brighter destiny can add nothing to that required something, which, so far as sociology can define it for us, we have seen to be so utterly inadequate. Social conditions, it is true, we may expect will go on improving; we may hope that the social machinery will come gradually to run more smoothly. But unless we know something positive to the contrary, the outcome of all this progress may be nothing but a more undisturbed ennui or a more soulless sensuality. The rose-leaves may be laid more smoothly, and yet the man that lies on them may be wearier or more degraded.

To-morrow, and to-morrow, and to-morrow
Creeps in this petty pace from day to day;
And all our yesterdays have lighted fools
The way to dusty death.
This, for all that sociology can inform us to the contrary, may be the lesson really taught us by the positive philosophy of progress.

But what the positivists themselves learn from it, is something very different. The following verses are George Eliot's:

Oh may I join the choir invisible
Of those immortal dead who live again
In lives made better by their presence. So
To live is heaven....
To make undying music in the world,
Breathing us beauteous order that controls
With growing sway the growing life of man.
So we inherit that sweet purity
For which we struggled, groaned, and agonised
With widening retrospect, that bred despair....
That better self shall live till human time
Shall fold its eyelids, and the human sky
Be gathered like a scroll within the tomb
Unread for ever. This is life to come,
Which martyred men have made more glorious

For us who strive to follow. May I reach
That purest heaven, and be to other souls
That cup of strength in some great agony,
Enkindle generous ardour, feed pure love,
Beget the smiles that have no cruelty,
Be the sweet presence of a good diffused,
And in diffusion ever more intense;
So shall I join that choir invisible
Whose music is the gladness of the world.

Here is the positive religion of benevolence and progress, as preached to the modern world in the name of exact thought, presented to us in an impassioned epitome. Here is hope, ardour, sympathy, and resolution, enough and to spare. The first question is,— How are these kindled, and what are they all about? They must, as we have seen, be about something that the science of sociology will not discover for us. Nor can they last, if, like an empty stomach, they prey only upon themselves. They must have some solid content, and the great thing needful is to discern this. It is quite true that to suffer, or even to die, will often seem dulce et decorum to a man; but it will only seem so when the end he dies or suffers for is, in his estimation, a worthy one. A Christian might be gladly crucified if by so doing he could turn men from vice to virtue; but a connoisseur in wine would not be crucified that his best friend might prefer dry champagne to sweet. All the agony and the struggles, then, that the positivist saint suffers with such enthusiasm, depend alike for their value and their possibility on the object that is supposed to cause them. And in the verses just quoted this object is indeed named several times; but it is named only incidentally and in vague terms, as if its nature and its value were self-evident, and could be left to take care of themselves; and the great thing to be dwelt upon were the means and not the end: whereas the former are really only the creatures of the latter, and can have no more honour than the latter is able to bestow upon them.

Now the only positive ends named in these verses are 'the better self,' 'sweet purity,' and 'smiles that have no cruelty.' The conditions of these are beauteous order,' and the result of them is the 'gladness of the world.' The rest of the language used adds nothing to our positive knowledge, but merely makes us feel the want of it. The purest heaven, we are told, that the men of any generation can look forward to, will be the increased gladness that their right conduct will secure for a coming generation: and that gladness, when it comes, will be, as it were, the seraphic song of the blessed and holy dead. Thus every present, for the positivist, is the future life of the past; earth is heaven perpetually realising itself; it is, as it were, an eternal choir-practice, in which the performers, though a little out of tune at present, are becoming momently more and more perfect. If this be so, there is a heaven of some sort about us at this moment. There is a musical gladness every day in our ears, our actual delight in which it might have been a heaven to our great-grandfathers to have anticipated in the last century.

Now it is plain that this alleged music is not everywhere. Where, then, is it? And will it, when we have found it, be found to merit all the praise that is bestowed upon it? Sociology, as we have seen, may show us how to secure to each performer his voice or his instrument; but it will not show us how to make either the voice or the instrument a good one; nor will it decide whether the orchestra shall perform Beethoven or Offenbach, or whether the chorus shall sing a penitential psalm or a drinking song. When we have discovered what the world's highest gladness can consist of, we will again come to the question of how far such gladness can be a general end of action.

[9] Vide Nineteenth Century, October, 1877.

[10] 'As Mr. Spencer points out, society does not resemble those organisms which are so highly centralised that the unity of the whole is the important thing, and every part must die if separated from the rest; but rather those that will bear separation and reunion; because, although there is a certain union and organisation of the parts in regard to one another, yet the far more important fact is the life of the parts separately. The true health of society depends upon the communes, the villages and townships, infinitely more than on the form and pageantry of an imperial government. If in them there is band-work, union for a common effort, converse in the working out of a common thought, there the Republic is.'—Professor Clifford, Nineteenth Century, October, 1877.

Is Life Worth Living? By William Hurrell Mallock

CHAPTER IV.

GOODNESS AS ITS OWN REWARD.

'Who chooses me must give, and hazard all he hath.' Inscription on the Leaden Casket. Merchant of Venice.

What I have been urging in the last chapter is really nothing more than the positivists admit themselves. It will be found, if we study their utterances as a whole, that they by no means believe practically in their own professions, or consider that the end of action can be either defined and verified by sociology, or made attractive by sympathy. On the contrary, they confess plainly how inadequate these are by themselves, by continually supplementing them with additions from quite another quarter. But their fault is that this confession is, apparently, only half conscious with them; and they are for ever reproducing arguments as sufficient which they have already in other moments implicitly condemned as meaningless. My aim has been, therefore, to put these arguments out of court altogether, and safely shut the doors on them. Hitherto they have played just the part of an idle populace, often turned out of doors, but as often breaking in again, and confusing with their noisy cheers a judgment that has not yet been given. Let us have done, then, with the conditions of happiness till we know what happiness is. Let us have done with enthusiasm till we know if there is anything to be enthusiastic about.

I have quoted George Eliot's cheers already, as expressing what this enthusiasm is. I will now quote her again, as showing how fully she recognises that its value depends upon its object, and that its only possible object must be of a definite, and in the first place, of a personal nature. In her novel of Daniel Deronda, the large part of the interest hangs on which way the heroine's character will develop itself; and this interest, in the opinion of the authoress, is of a very intense kind. Why should it be? she asks explicitly. And she gives her answer in the following very remarkable and very instructive passage:

'Could there be a slenderer, more insignificant thread,' she says, 'in human history, than this consciousness of a girl, busy with her small inferences of the way in which she could make her life pleasant? in a time too, when ideas were with fresh vigour making armies of themselves, and the universal kinship was declaring itself fiercely: when women on the other side of the world would not mourn for the husbands and sons who died bravely in a common cause; and men, stinted of bread, on one side of the world, heard of that willing loss and were patient; a time when the soul of man was waking the pulses which had for centuries been beating in him unheard, until their full sense made a new life of terror or of joy.

'What in the midst of that mighty drama are girls and their blind visions? They are the Yea or Nay of that good for which men are enduring and fighting. In these delicate vessels is borne onward through the ages the treasure of human affections.'

Now here we come to solid ground at last. Here is an emphatic and frank admission of all that I was urging in the last chapter; and the required end of action and test of conduct is brought to a focus and localized. It is not described, it is true; but a narrow circle is drawn round it, and our future search for it becomes a matter of comparative ease. We are in a position now to decide whether it exists, or does not exist. It consists primarily and before all things in the choice by the individual of one out of many modes of happiness—the election of a certain 'way,' in George Eliot's words, 'in which he will make his life pleasant.' There are many sets of pleasure open to him; but there is one set, it is said, more excellent, beyond comparison, than the others; and to choose these, and these alone, is what will give us part in the holy value of life. The choice and the refusal of them is the Yea and the Nay of all that makes life worth living; and is the source, to the positivists, of the solemnity, the terrors, and sweetness of the whole ethical vocabulary. 'What then are the alternative pleasures that life offers me? In how many ways am I capable of feeling my existence a blessing? and in what way shall I feel the blessing of it most keenly?' This is the great life-question; it may be asked indifferently by any individual; and in the positivist answer to it, which will be the same for all, and of universal application, must lie the foundation of the positive moral system.

And that system, as I have said before, professes to be essentially a moral one, in the old religious sense of the word. It retains the old ethical vocabulary; and lays the same intense stress on the old ethical distinctions. Nor is this a mere profession only. We shall see that the system logically requires it. One of its chief virtues—indeed the only virtue in it we have defined hitherto—is, as has been seen, an habitual self-denial. But a denial of what? Of something, plainly, that if denied to ourselves, can be conveyed as a negative or positive good to others. But the good things that are thus transferable cannot plainly be the 'highest good,' or morality would consist largely of a surrender of its own end. This end must evidently be something inward and inalienable, just as the religious end was. It is a certain inward state of the heart, and of the heart's affections. For this inward state to be fully produced, and maintained generally, a certain sufficiency of material well-being may be requisite; but without this inward state such sufficiency will be morally valueless. Day by day we must of course have our daily bread. But the positivists must maintain, just as the Christians did, that man does not live by bread alone; and that his life does not consist in the abundance of the things that he possesses. And thus when they are brought face to face with the matter, we find them all, with one consent, condemning as false the same allurements that were condemned by Christianity; and pointing, as it did, to some other treasure that will not wax old—some water, the man who drinks of which will never thirst more.

Now what is this treasure—this inward state of the heart? What is its analysis, and why is it so precious? As yet we are quite in the dark as to this. No positive moralist has as yet shown us, in any satisfactory way, either of these things. This statement, I know, will be contradicted by many; and, until it is explained further, it is only natural that it should be. It will be said that a positive human happiness of just the kind needed has been put before the world again and again; and not only put before it, but earnestly followed and reverently enjoyed by many. Have not truth, benevolence, purity, and, above all, pure affection, been, to many, positive ends of action for their own sakes, without any thought, as Dr. Tyndall says, 'of any reward or punishment looming in the future'? Is not virtue followed in the noblest way, when its followers, if asked what reward they look for, can say to it, as Thomas Aquinas said to Christ, 'Nil nisi te, Domine'? And has not it so been followed? and is not the positivist position, to a large extent at any rate, proved?

Is it not true, as has been said by a recent writer, that[11] 'lives nourished, and invigorated by [a purely human] ideal have been, and still may be, seen amongst us, and the appearance of but a single example proves the adequacy of the belief?'

I reply that the fact is entirely true, and the inference entirely false. And this brings me at once to a point I have before alluded to—to the most subtle source of the entire positivist error—the source secret and unsuspected, of so much rash confidence.

The positive school can, and do, as we have seen, point to certain things in life which have every appearance, at first sight, of adequate moral ends. Their adequacy seems to be verified by every right feeling, and also by practical experiment. But there is one great fact that is forgotten. The positive school, when they deal with life, profess to exhibit its resources to us wholly free from the false aids of religion. They profess (if I may coin a word) to have de-religionized it before they deal with it. But about this matter they betray a most strange ignorance. They think the task is far simpler than it is. They seem to look on religion as existing nowhere except in its pure form, in the form of distinct devotional feeling, or in the conscious assents of faith; and, these once got rid of, they fancy that life is de-religionized. But the process thus far is really only begun; indeed, as far as immediate results go, it is hardly even begun; for it is really but a very small proportion of religion that exists pure. The greater part of it has entered into combination with the acts and feelings of life, thus forming as it were, a kind of amalgam with them, giving them new properties, a new colour, a new consistence. To de-religionize life, then, it is not enough to condemn creeds and to abolish prayers. We must further sublimate the beliefs and feelings, which prayers and creeds hold pure, out of the lay life around us. Under this process, even if imperfectly performed, it will soon become clear that religion in greater or less proportions is lurking everywhere. We shall see it yielded up even by things in which we should least look for it—by wit, by humour, by secular ambition, by most forms of vice, and by our daily light amusements. Much more shall we see it yielded up by heroism, by purity, by affection, and by love of truth—by all those things that the positivists most specially praise.

The positivists think, it would seem, that they had but to kill God, and that his inheritance shall be ours. They strike out accordingly the theistic beliefs in question, and then turn instantly to life: they sort its resources, count its treasures, and then say, 'Aim at this, and this, and this. See how beautiful is holiness; see how rapturous is pleasure. Surely these are worth seeking for their own sakes, without any "reward or punishment looming in the future."' They find, in fact, the interests and the sentiments of the world's present life—all the glow and all the gloom of it—lying before them like the colours on a painter's palette, and think they have nothing to do but set to work and use them. But let them wait a moment; they are in far too great a hurry. The palette and its colours are not nearly ready for them.

One of the colours of life—religion, that is—a colour which, by their own admission, has been hitherto an important one, they have swept clean away. They have swept it clean away, and let them remember why they have done so. It may be a pleasing colour, or it may not: that is a matter of taste. But the reason why it is to be got rid of is that it is not a fast colour. It is found to fade instantly in the spreading sunlight of knowledge. It is rapidly getting dim and dull and dead. When once it is gone, we shall never be able to restore it, and our future pictures of life must be tinted without its aid. They therefore profess loudly that they will employ it no longer.

But there is this point, this all-important point, that quite escapes them. They sweep the colour, in its pure state, clean off the palette; and then profess to show us by experiment that they can get on perfectly well without it. But they never seem to suspect that it may be mixed up with the colours they retain, and be the secret of their depth and lustre. Let them see whether religion be not lurking there, as a subtle colouring principle in all their pigments, even a grain of it producing effects that else were quite impossible. Let them only begin this analysis, and it will very soon be clear to them that to cleanse life of religion is not so simple a process as they seem to fancy it. Its actual dogmas may be readily put away from us; not so the effect which these dogmas have worked during the course of centuries. In disguised forms they are around us everywhere; they confront us in every human interest, in every human pleasure. They have beaten themselves into life; they have eaten their way into it. Like a secret sap they have flavoured every fruit in the garden. They are like a powerful drug, a stimulant, that has been injected into our whole system.

If then we could appraise the vigour and value of life independent of religion, we can draw no direct conclusions from observing it in its present state. Before such observations can teach us anything, there is a great deal that will have to be made allowance for: and the positive school, when they reason from life as it is, are building therefore on an utterly unsound foundation. It is emphatically untrue to say that a single example in the present day, or for matter of that any number of examples, either goes or can go any way towards proving the adequacy of any non-religious formula. For all such formulæ have first to be further analysed before we know how far they are really non-religious; and secondly the religious element that will be certainly found existing in them will have, hypothetically, to be removed.

It would be well if the positive school would spend in this spiritual analysis but a little of that skill they have attained to in their analysis of matter. In their experiments, for instance, on spontaneous generation, what untold pains have been taken! With what laborious thought, with what emulous ingenuity, have they struggled to completely sterilise the fluids in which they are to seek for the new production of life! How jealously do they guard against leaving there any already existing germs! How easily do they tell us their experiments may be vitiated by the smallest oversight!

Surely spiritual matters are worthy of an equally careful treatment. For what we have here to study is not the production of the lowest forms of animal life, but the highest forms of human happiness. These were once thought to be always due to religion. The modern doctrine is that they are producible without such aid. Let us treat, then, the beauty of holiness, the love of truth, 'the treasure of human affection,' and so forth, as Dr. Tyndall has treated the infusions in which life is said to originate. Let us boil them down, so to speak, and destroy every germ of religion in them, and then see how far they will generate the same ecstatic happiness. And let us treat in this way vice no less than virtue. Having once done this, we may honestly claim whatever yet remains to us. Then, we shall see what materials of happiness we can, as positive thinkers, call our own. Then, a positive moral system, if any such be possible, will begin to have a real value for us—then, but not till then.

Such an analysis as this must be naturally a work of time; and much of it must be performed by each one of us for ourselves. But a sample of the operation can be given here, which will show plainly enough its nature, and the ultimate results of it. I shall begin, for this purpose, with reconsidering the moral end generally, and the three primary characteristics that are ascribed, by all parties, to it, as essentials. I shall point out, generally also, how much of religion is embodied in all these; and shall then proceed to one or two concrete examples, taken from the pleasures and passions that animate the life around us.

These three characteristics of the moral end are its inwardness, its importance, and, within certain limits, its absolute character.

I begin with its inwardness. I have spoken of this several times already, but the matter is so important that it will well bear repetition. By calling the moral end inward, I mean that it resides primarily not in action, but in motives to action; in the will, not in the deed; not in what we actually do, but in what we actually endeavour to do; in the love we give, rather than in the love that we receive. What defiles a man is that which comes out of his heart—evil thoughts, murders, adulteries. The thoughts may never find utterance in a word, the murders and adulteries may never be fulfilled in act; and yet, if a man be restrained, not by his own will, but only by outer circumstances, his immorality will be the same. The primary things we are 'responsible for,' observes a recent positive writer,[12] are 'frames of mind into which we knowingly and willingly work ourselves': and when these are once wrong, he adds, 'they are wrong for ever: no accidental failure of their good or evil fruits can possibly alter that.' And as with what is wrong or vicious, so with what is right or virtuous; this in a like manner proceeds out of the mind or heart. 'The gladness of true heroism,' says Dr. Tyndall, 'visits the heart of him who is really competent to say, "I court truth."' It is not, be it observed, the objective attainment of truth that creates the gladness. It is the subjective desire, the subjective resolution. The moral end, for the positivist just as much as for the believer, is a certain inward state of the heart, or mind—a state which will of necessity, if possible, express itself in action, but whose value is not to be measured by the success of that expression. The battle-ground of good and evil is within us; and the great human event is the issue of the struggle between them.

And this leads us on to the second point. The language used on all hands respecting this struggle, implies that its issue is of an importance great out of all proportion to our own consciousness of the results of it, nay, even that it is independent of our consciousness. It is implied that though a man may be quite ignorant of the state of his own heart, and though no one else can so much as guess at it, what that state is is of great and peculiar moment. If this were not so, and the importance of our inner state had reference only to our own feelings about it, self-deception would be as good as virtue. To believe we were upright, pure, and benevolent would be as good as to be so. We might have all the pleasures of morality with none of its inconveniences; for it is easy, if I may borrow a phrase of Mr. Tennyson's, to become so false that we take ourselves for true; and thus, tested by any pain or joy that we ourselves were conscious of, the results of the completest falsehood would be the same as those of the completest virtue.

But let a man be never so perfect an instance of a result like this, no positivist moralist would contend that he was virtuous, or that he could be said, at his death, to have found the true treasure of life. On the contrary his career would be regarded as, in the profoundest sense, a tragedy. It is for this reason that such a value is set at present upon feminine purity, and that we are accustomed to call the woman ruined that has lost it. The outer harm done may not be great, and may lead to no ill consequences. The harm is all within: the tragedy is in the soul itself. But—and this is more important still—even here the harm may not be recognised: the act in question may lead to no remorse; and yet despite this, the case will be made no better. On the contrary it will be made a great deal worse. Any father or husband would recognise this, who was not professedly careless about all moral matters altogether. It would not, for instance, console a positivist for his daughter's seduction to know that the matter was hushed up, and that it gave the lady herself no concern whatever. It is implied in the language of all who profess to regard morality, that whether the guilty person be conscious or no of any remorse or sorrow, the same harm has been done by what we call guilt.

There is, however (and this brings us to the third point), a very large part of the world that, as a fact, no matter what it professes, really sets upon morality no true value whatever. If it has ever realised at all what morality is, it has done so only partially; it has been more impressed with its drawbacks than with its attractions, and it becomes practically happier and more contented, the more it forgets the very idea of virtue. But it is implied, as we have seen, in the usual language of all of us that, let the vicious be as happy as possible, they have no right to such a happiness, and that if they choose to take it, it will in some way or other be the worse for them. This language evidently implies farther that there is some standard by which happiness is to be measured, quite apart from its completeness, and from our individual desire for it. That standard is something absolute, beyond and above the taste of any single man or of any body of men. It is a standard to which the human race can be authoritatively ordered to conform, or be despised, derided, and hated, if it refuse to do so. It is implied that those who find their happiness in virtue have a right to order and to force, if possible, all others to do the same. Unless we believed this there would be no such thing as moral earnestness in the propagation of any system. There could, indeed, be no such thing as propagandism at all. If a man (to use an example of Mill's) preferred to be a contented pig rather than a discontented Socrates, we should have no positive reason for thinking him wrong; even did we think so we should have no motive for telling him so; even if we told him, we should have no means of convincing him.

Those, then, who regard morality as the rule of action, and the one key that can unlock for each of us the true treasure of life, who talk of things being noble and sacred and heroic, who call our responsibilities and our privileges[13] awful, and who urge on a listless world the earnestness and the solemnity of existence—all those, I say, who use such language as this, imply of the moral end three necessary things: first, that its essence is inward, in the heart of man; secondly, that its value is incalculable, and its attainment the only true happiness for us; thirdly, that its standard is something absolute, and not in the competence of any man or of all men to alter or abolish. That this is true may be very easily seen. Deny any one of these propositions; say that the moral end consists in something outward and alienable, not in something inward and inalienable; that its importance is small, and second to many other things; that its standard is not absolute, but varies according to individual taste; and morality becomes at once impossible to preach, and not worth preaching.

Now for all these characteristics of the end of life, the theism that modern thought is rejecting could offer a strictly logical basis. And first, as to its importance. Here it may be said, certainly, that theism cuts the knot, and does not untie it. But at all events it gets rid of it; and in the following way. The theist confesses freely that the importance of the moral end is a thing that the facts of life, as we now know them, will never properly explain to us. It can at present be divined and augured only; its value is one of promise rather than of performance; and the possession itself is a thing that passes understanding. It belongs to a region of mystery into which neither logic nor experiment will ever suffice to carry us; and whose secrets are beyond the reach of any intellectual aeronaut. But it is a part of the theistic creed that such a region is; and that the things that pass understanding are the most important things of life. Nothing would be gained, however, by postulating merely a mystery—an unknowable. This must be so far known by the theist, that he knows its connection with himself. He must know, too, that if this connection is to have any effect on him, it must be not merely temporary, but permanent and indissoluble. Such a connection he finds in his two distinctive doctrines—the existence of a personal God, which gives him the connection; and his own personal immortality, which perpetuates it. Thus the theist, upon his own theory, has an eye ever upon him. He is in constant relationship with a conscious omnipotent Being, in whose likeness he is in some sort formed, and to which he is in some sort kin. To none of his actions is this Being indifferent; and with this Being his relations for good or evil will never cease. Thus, though he may not realise their true nature now, though he may not realise how infinitely good the good is, or how infinitely evil the evil, there is a day in store for him when his eyes will be opened, and what he now sees only through a glass darkly, he will see face to face.

The objectivity of the moral end—or rather the objective standard of the subjective end—is explained in the same way. The standard is God's will, not man's immediate happiness. And yet to this will, as soon as, by natural or supernatural means, we discern it, the Godlike part of our nature at once responds: it at once acknowledges it as eternal and divine, although we can give no logical reasons for such acknowledgment.

By the light, too, of these same beliefs, the inwardness of the moral end assumes an explicable meaning. Man's primary duty is towards God; his secondary duty is towards his brother men; and it is only from the filial relation that the fraternal springs. The moral end, then, is so precious in the eyes of the theist, because the inward state that it consists of is agreeable to what God wills—a God who reads the heart, and who cannot be deceived. And the theist's peace or gladness in his highest moral actions springs not so much from the consciousness of what he does or is, as of the reasons why he does or is it—reasons that reach far away beyond the earth and its destinies, and connect him with some timeless and holy mystery.

Thus theism, whether it be true or no, can give a logical and a full account of the supposed nature of the moral end, and of its supposed importance. Let us turn now to positivism, and consider what is its position. The positivist, we must remember, conceives of the moral end in the same way, and sets upon it the same value. Let us see how far his own premisses will give him any support in this. These premisses, so far as they differ from those of theism, consist of two great denials: there is no personal God, and there is no personal immortality. We will glance rapidly at the direct results of these.

In the first place, they confine all the life with which we can have the least moral connection to the surface of this earth, and to the limited time for which life and consciousness can exist upon it. They isolate the moral law, as I shall show more clearly hereafter, from any law or force in the universe that may be wider and more permanent. When the individual dies, he can only be said to live by metaphor, in the results of his outward actions. When the race dies, in no thinkable way can we say that it will live at all. Everything will then be as though it never had been. Whatever humanity may have done before its end arrives, however high it may have raised itself, however low it may have sunk itself,

The event
Will trammel up the consequence, and catch
With its success surcease.

All the vice of the world, and all its virtue, all its pleasures and all its pains, will have effected nothing. They will all have faded like an unsubstantial pageant, and not left a wrack behind.

Here, then, the importance of morality at once changes both its dimensions and its kind. It is confined within narrow limitations of space and time. It is no longer a thing we can talk vaguely about, or to which any sounding but indefinite phrases will be applicable. We can no longer say either to the individual or the race,

Choose well, and your choice is
Brief, but yet endless.[14]

We can only say that it is brief, and that bye and bye what it was will be no matter to anyone.

Still within these limits it may be said, certainly, that it is a great thing for us that we should be happy; and if it be true that the moral end brings the greatest happiness, then it is man's greatest achievement to attain to the moral end. But when we say that the greatest happiness resides in the moral end, we must be careful to see what it is we mean. We may mean that as a matter of fact men generally give a full assent to this, and act accordingly, which is the most obvious falsehood that could be uttered on any subject; or we may mean—indeed, if we mean anything we must mean—that they would give a full assent, and act accordingly, could their present state of mind undergo a complete change, and their eyes be opened, which at present are fast closed. But according to the positivist theory, this hypothesis is in most cases an impossibility. The moral end, as we have seen, is an inward state of the heart; and the heart, on the showing of the positivists, is for each man an absolute solitude. No one can gain admission to it but by his assistance; and to the larger part no one can ever gain admission at all.

Thus in the seas of life enisled,
With echoing straits between us thrown,
Dotting the shoreless watery wild,
We mortal myriads live alone.
So says Mr. Matthew Arnold; and the gentle Keble utters the same sentiment, remarking, with a delicate pathos, how seldom those even who have known us best and longest

Know half the reason why we smile or sigh.
Thus in the recesses of his own soul each man is, for the positivist, as much alone as if he were the only conscious thing in the universe; and his whole inner life, when he dies, will, to use some words of George Eliot's that I have already quoted,

Be gathered like a scroll within the tomb,
Unread for ever.
No one shall enquire into his inward thoughts, much less shall anyone judge him for them. To no one except himself can he in any way have to answer for them.

Such is the condition of the individual according to the positivist theory. It is evident, therefore, that one of the first results of positivism is to destroy even the rudiments of any machinery by which one man could govern, with authority, the inward kingdom of another; and the moral imperative is reduced to an empty vaunt. For what can be an emptier flourish than for one set of men, and these a confessed minority, to proclaim imperious laws to others, which they can never get the others to obey, and which are essentially meaningless to the only people to whom they are not superfluous? Suppose that, on positive grounds, I find pleasure in humility, and my friend finds pleasure in pride, and so far as we can form a judgment the happiness of us both is equal; what possible grounds can I have for calling my state better than his? Were I a theist, I should have the best of grounds, for I should believe that hereafter my friend's present contentment would be dissipated, and would give place to despair. But as a positivist, if his contentment do but last his lifetime, what can I say except this, that he has chosen what, for him, was his better part for ever, and no God or man will ever take it away from him? To say then that his immoral state was worse than my moral state would be a phrase incapable of any practical meaning. It might mean that, could my friend be made to think as I do, he would be happier than he is at present; but we have here an impossible hypothesis, and an unverifiable conclusion. It is true enough that I might present to my friend some image of my own inward state, and of all the happiness it gave me; but if, having compared his happiness and mine as well as he could, he still liked his own best, exhortation would have no power, and reproach no meaning.

Here, then, are three results—simple, immediate, and necessary—of positivism, on the moral end. Of the three characteristics at present supposed essential to it, positivism eliminates two and materially modifies the third.

In the first place, the importance of the moral end is altogether changed in character. It has nothing in it whatever of the infinite, and a scientific forecast can already see the end of it.

In the second place, it is nothing absolute, and not being absolute is incapable of being enforced.

In the third place, its value, such as it is, is measured only by the conscious happiness that its possession gives us, or the conscious pains that its loss gives us.

Still it may be contended with plausibility that the moral end, when once seen, is sufficient to attract us by its own inalienable charm, and can hold its own independently of any further theories as to its nature and its universality. It remains now to come to practical life, and see if this really be so; to see if the pleasures in life that are supposed the highest will not lose their attractiveness when robbed of the three characteristics of which the positive theory robs them.

Is Life Worth Living? By William Hurrell Mallock

CHAPTER V.

LOVE AS A TEST OF GOODNESS.

Ερωτα δε, τον τυραννον ανδρων,
Τον τας Αφροδιτας
Φιλτατων θαλαμων
Κληδουχον, ου σεβιζομεν,
Περθοντα.—Euripides.

I will again re-state, in other words than my own, the theory we are now going to test by the actual facts of life. 'The assertion,' says Professor Huxley, 'that morality is in any way dependent on certain philosophical problems, produces the same effect on my mind as if one should say that a man's vision depends on his theory of sight, or that he has no business to be sure that ginger is hot in his mouth, unless he has formed definite views as to the nature of ginger.' Or, to put the matter in slightly different language, the sorts of happiness, we are told, that are secured to us by moral conduct are facts, so far as regards our own consciousness of them, as simple, as constant and as universal, as is the perception of the outer world secured to us by our eyesight, or as the sensation formed on the palate by the application of ginger to it.

Love, for instance, according to this view, is as simple a delight for men in its highest forms as it is for animals in its lowest. What George Eliot calls 'the treasure of human affection' depends as little for its value on any beliefs outside itself as does the treasure of animal appetite; and just as no want of religious faith can deprive the animals of the last, so no want of religious faith can deprive mankind of the first. It will remain a stable possession to us, amid the wreck of creeds, giving life a solemn and intense value of its own. It will never fail us as a sure test of conduct. Whatever guides us to this treasure we shall know is moral; whatever tends to withdraw us from it we shall know is immoral.

Such is the positivist theory as to all the higher pleasures of life, of which affection confessedly is one of the chief, and also the most obviously human. Let us proceed now from generalities to special concrete facts, and see how far this theory is borne out by them. And we can find none better than those which are now before us—the special concrete facts of affection, and of sexual affection in particular.

The affection of man for woman—or, as it will be best to call it, love—has been ever since time was, one of the chief elements in the life of man. But it was not till Christianity had very fully developed itself that it assumed the peculiar importance that is now claimed for it. For the ancient world it was a passion sure to come to most men, and that would bring joy or sorrow to them as the case might be. The worldly wisdom of some convinced them that it gave more joy than sorrow; so they took and used it as long as it chanced to please them. The worldly wisdom of others convinced them that it gave more sorrow than joy, so they did all they could, like Lucretius, to school themselves into a contempt for it. But for the modern world it is on quite a different footing, and its value does not depend on such a chance balance of pains and pleasures. The latter are not of the same nature as the former, and so cannot be outweighed by them. In the judgment of the modern world,

'Tis better to have loved and lost
Than never to have loved at all.

To love, in fact, though not exactly said to be incumbent upon all men, is yet endowed with something that is almost of the nature of a duty. If a man cannot love, it is looked on as a sort of moral misfortune, if not as a moral fault in him. And when a man can love, and does love successfully, then it is held that his whole nature has burst out into blossom. The imaginative literature of the modern world centres chiefly about this human crisis; and its importance in literature is but a reflection of its importance in life. It is, as it were, the sun of the world of sentiment—the source of its lights and colours, and also of its shadows. It is the crown of man's existence; it gives life its highest quality; and, if we can believe what those who have known it tell us, earth under its influence seems to be melting into, and to be almost joined with, heaven.

All this language, however, about love, no matter how true in a certain sense it may be, is emphatically true about it in a certain sense only, and is by no means to be taken without reserve. It is emphatically not true about love in general, but only about love as modified in a certain special way. The form of the affection, so to speak, is more important than the substance of it. It will need but little consideration to show us that this is so. Love is a thing that can take countless forms; and were not the form, for the modern world, the thing of the first importance, the praise bestowed upon all forms of it would be equal, or graduated only with reference to intensity. But the very reverse of this is the case really. In our estimate of an affection, its intensity, though doubtless of great importance, is yet of an importance that is clearly secondary. Else things that the modern world regards as the most abominable might be on a level with the things it regards as most pure and holy; the lovers of Athens might even put to shame with their passion the calm sacramental constancy of many a Christian pair; and the whole fabric of modern morals would be undermined. For, according to the modern conception of morals, love can not only give life its highest quality, but its lowest also. If it can raise man to the angels, it can also sink him below the beasts; and as to its intensity, it is a force which will carry him in the one direction just as well as the other. Kind and not degree is the first thing needful. It is the former, and not the latter, that essentially separates David and Jonathan from Harmodius and Aristogeiton, St. Elizabeth from Cleopatra, the beloved disciple from Antinous. How shall we love? is the great question for us. It comes long before, How much shall we love?

Let us imagine a bride and bridegroom of the type that would now be most highly reverenced, and try to understand something of what their affection is. It is, of course, impossible here to treat such a subject adequately; for, as Mr. Carlyle says, 'except musically, and in the language of poetry, it can hardly be so much as spoken about.' But enough for the present purpose can perhaps be said. In the first place, then, the affection in question will be seen to rest mainly upon two things—firstly, on the consciousness of their own respective characters on the part of each; and, secondly, on the idea formed by each of the character of the other. Each must have a faith, for instance, in his or her own purity, and each must have a like faith, also in the purity of the other. Thus, to begin with the first requisites, a man can only love a woman in the highest sense when he does so with a perfectly clear conscience. There must be no obstacle between them which shocks his sense of right, or which, if known by the woman, would shock hers. Were the affection indulged in, in spite of such an obstacle, its fine quality would be injured, no matter how great its intensity; and, instead of a moral blessing, it would become a moral curse. An exquisite expression of the necessity of this personal sense of rightness may be read into the well-known lines,

I could not love thee, dear, so well,
Loved I not honour more.
Nor shall we look on honour here as having reference only to external acts and conditions. It has reference equally, if not more, to the inward state of the heart. The man must be conscious not only that he is loving the right woman, but that he is loving her in the right way. 'If I loved not purity more than you,' he would say to her, 'I were not worthy of you.'

And further, just as he requires to possess this taintless conscience himself, so does he require to be assured that the like is possessed by her. Unless he knows that she loves purity more than him, there is no meaning in his aspiration that he may be found worthy of her. The gift of her affection that is of such value to him, is not of value because it is affection simply, but because it is affection of a high kind; and its elevation is of more consequence to him than its intensity, or even than its continuance. He would sooner that at the expense of its intensity it remained pure, than that at the expense of its purity it remained intense. Othello was certainly not a husband of the highest type, and yet we see something of this even in his case. His sufferings at his wife's supposed inconstancy have doubtless in them a large selfish element. Much of them is caused by the mere passion of jealousy. But the deepest sting of all does not lie here. It lies rather in the thought of what his wife has done to herself, than of what she has done to him. This is what overcomes him.

> The bawdy wind, that kisses all it meets,
> Is hushed within the hollow mine of earth,
> And will not hear it.

He could have borne anything but a soul's tragedy like this:

> Alas! to make me
> A fixed figure for the time of scorn
> To point his slow unmoving finger at!
> Yet I could bear that too, well—very well:
> But there, where I have garnered up my heart,
> Where I must either live, or bear no life;
> The fountain from the which my current runs
> Or else dries up; to be discarded thence!
> Or keep it as a cistern for foul toads
> To knot and gender in!

Whenever he was with her, Desdemona might still be devoted to him. She might only give to Cassio what she could not give to her husband. But to Othello this would be no comfort. The fountain would be polluted 'from which his current runs'; and though its waters might still flow for him, he would not care to touch them. If this feeling is manifest in such a love as Othello's, much more is it manifest in love of a higher type. It is expressed thus, for instance, by the heroine of Mrs. Craven's 'Récit d'une Sœur.' 'I can indeed say,' she says, 'that we never loved each other so much as when we saw how we both loved God:' and again, 'My husband would not have loved me as he did, if he had not loved God a great deal more.' This language is of course distinctly religious; but it embodies a meaning that is appreciated by the positive school as well. In positivist language it might be expressed thus: 'My husband would not have loved me as he did, if he would not, sooner than love me in any other way, have ceased to love me altogether.' It is clear that this sentiment is proper, nay essential, to positivist affection, just as well as to Christian. Any pure and exalted love would at once change its character, if, without any further change, it merely believed it were free to change it. Its strongest element is the consciousness, not that it is of such a character only, but that this character is the right one. The ideal bride and bridegroom, the ideal man and wife, would not value purity as they are supposed to do, did they not believe that it was not only different from impurity, but essentially and incalculably better than it. For the positivist, just as much as the Christian, this sense of rightness in love is interfused with the affection proper, and does as it were give wings to it. It far more than makes good for the lovers any loss of intensity that may be created by the chastening down of passion:

and figuratively at least, it may be said to make them conscious that 'underneath them are the everlasting arms.'

Here then in love, as the positive school at present offer it to us, are all these three characteristics to which that school, as we have seen, must renounce all right. It is characterised as conforming to some special and absolute standard, of which no positive account can be given; the conformity is inward, and so cannot be enforced; and for all that positive knowledge can show us, its importance may be a dream.

We shall realise this better if we consider a love from which these three characteristics have, as far as possible, been abstracted—a love which professes 110frankly to rest upon its own attractions, and which repudiates all such epithets as worse or better. This will at once show us not only of what various developments the passion of love is capable, but also how false it is to imagine that the highest kind need naturally be the most attractive.

I have quoted Othello, and Mrs. Craven's heroine as types of love when religionized. We will go to the modern Parisian school for the type of love when de-religionized—a school which, starting from the same premisses as do the positive moralists, yet come to a practical teaching that is singularly different. And let us remember that just as the ideal we have been considering already, is the ideal most ardently looked to by one part of the world, so is the ideal we are going to consider now, looked to with an equal ardour by another part of the world. The writer in particular from whom I am about to quote has been one of the most popular of all modern romancers; and has been hailed by men of the most fastidious culture as a preacher to these latter generations of a bolder and more worthy gospel. 'This,'15 says one of the best known of our living poets, of the work that I select to quote from—

This is the golden book of spirit and sense,
The holy writ of beauty.
111Of this 'holy writ' the chief theme is love. Let us go on to see how love is there presented to us.

'You know,' says Théophile Gautier's best-known hero, in a letter to a friend, 'you know the eagerness with which I have sought for physical beauty, the importance I attach to outward form, and how the world I am in love with is the world that the eyes can see: or to put the matter in more conventional language, I am so corrupt and blasé that my faith in moral beauty is gone, and my power of striving after it also. I have lost the faculty to discern between good and evil, and this loss has well nigh brought me back to the ignorance of the child or savage. To tell the plain truth, nothing seems to me to be worthy either of praise or blame, and I am but little perturbed by even the most abnormal actions. My conscience is deaf and dumb. Adultery seems to me the most commonplace thing possible. I see nothing shocking in a young girl selling herself.'... 'I find that the earth is all as fair as heaven, and virtue for me is nothing but the perfection of form.' 'Many a time and long', he continues farther on, 'have I paused in some cathedral, under the shadow of the marble foliage, when the lights were quivering in through the stained windows, when the organ unbidden made a low murmuring of itself, and the wind was breathing amongst the pipes; and I have plunged my gaze far into the pale blue depths112 of the almond-shaped eyes of the Madonna. I have followed with a tender reverence the curves of that wasted figure of hers, and the arch of her eyebrows, just visible and no more than that. I have admired her smooth and lustrous brow, her temples with their transparent chastity, and her cheeks shaded with a sober virginal colour, more tender than the colour of a peach-flower. I have counted one by one the fair and golden lashes that threw their tremulous shade upon it. I have traced out with care in the subdued tone that surrounds her, the evanescent lines of her throat, so fragile and inclined so modestly. I have even lifted with an adventuring hand the folds of her tunic, and have seen unveiled that bosom, maiden and full of milk, that has never been pressed by any except divine lips. I have traced out the rare clear veins of it, even to their faintest branchings. I have laid my finger on it, to draw the white drops forth, of the draught of heaven. I have so much as touched with my lips the very bud of the rosa mystica.

'Well, and I confess it honestly, all this immaterial beauty, this thing so winged and so aerial that one knows well enough it is soon going to fly away from one, has never moved me to any great degree. I love the Venus Anadyomene better, better a thousand times. These old-world eyes, slightly raised at the corners! these lips so pure and so113 firmly chiselled, so amorous, and so fit for kissing! this low, broad brow! these tresses with the curves in them of the sea water, and bound behind her head in a knot, negligently! these firm and shining shoulders! this back, with its thousand alluring contours! all these fair and rounded outlines, this air of superhuman vigour in a body so divinely feminine—all this enraptures and enchants me in a way of which you can have no idea—you the Christian and the philosopher.

'Mary, despite the humble air affected by her, is a deal too haughty for me. It is as much as her foot does, swathed in its white coverings, if it just touches the earth, now purpling where the old serpent writhes. Her eyes are the loveliest eyes in the world; but they are always turned heavenwards, or else they are cast down. They never look you straight in the face. They have never served as the mirror of a human form.... Venus comes, from the sea to take possession of the world, as a goddess who loves men should—quite naked and quite alone. Earth is more to her liking than is Olympus, and amongst her lovers she has more men than gods. She drapes herself in no faint veils of mystery. She stands straight upright, her dolphin behind her, and her foot upon her opal-coloured shell. The sun strikes full upon her smooth limbs, and her white hand holds in air the waves of her[114] fair locks, which old father Ocean has sprinkled with his most perfect pearls. One can see her. She hides nothing; for modesty was only made for those who have no beauty. It is an invention of the modern world; the child of the Christian contempt for form and matter.

'Oh ancient world! all that you held in reverence is held in scorn by us. Thine idols are overthrown in the dust; fleshless anchorites clad in rags and tatters, martyrs with the blood fresh on them, and their shoulders torn by the tigers of thy circuses, have perched themselves on the pedestals of thy fair desirable gods. The Christ has enveloped the whole world in his winding-sheet.... Oh purity, plant of bitterness, born on a blood-soaked soil, and whose degenerate and sickly blossom expands with difficulty in the dank shade of cloisters, under a chill baptismal rain; rose without scent, and spiked all round with thorns, thou hast taken the place for us of the glad and gracious roses, bathed with nard and wine, of the dancing girls of Sybaris!

'The ancient world knew thee not, oh sterile flower! thou wast never enwoven in its chaplets of delirious perfume. In that vigorous and healthy society they would have spurned thee under foot disdainfully. Purity, mysticism, melancholy—three words unknown to thee, three new maladies brought into our life by the Christ!... For me,[115] I look on woman in the old world manner, like a fair slave, made only for our pleasures. Christianity, in my eyes, has done nothing to rehabilitate her.... To say the truth, I cannot conceive for what reason there should be this desire in woman to be looked on as on a level with men.... I have made some love-verses in my time, or at least something that aspired to pass for such ... and there is not a vestige in them of the modern feeling of love.... There is nothing there, as in all the love-poetry since the Christian era, of a soul which, because it loves, begs another soul to love it back again; nothing there of a blue and shining lake, which begs a stream to pour itself into its bosom, that both together they may mirror the stars of heaven; nothing there of a pair of ring-doves, opening their wings together, that they may both together fly to the same nest.'[16]

Such is the account the hero gives of the nature of his love for woman. Nor does he give this account regretfully, or think that it shows him to be in any diseased condition. It shows rather a return, on his part, to a health that others have lost. As he looks round upon the modern world and the purity that George Eliot says in her verses she would die for, 'Woman,' he exclaims mournfully, 'is become the symbol of moral and physical beauty. The real fall of man was on the birthday of [116]the babe of Bethlehem.'[17] It will be instructive to notice further that these views are carried out by him to their full legitimate consequences, even though this, to some degree, is against his will. 'Sometimes,' he says, 'I try to persuade myself that such passions are abominable, and I say as much to myself in as severe a way as I can. But the words come only from my lips. They are arguments that I make. They are not arguments that I feel. The thing in question really seems quite natural to me, and anyone else in my place would, it seems to me, do as I do.'18

Nor is this conception of love peculiar to the hero only. The heroine's conception is its exact counterpart, and exactly fits it. The heroine as completely as the hero has freed herself from any discernment between good and evil. She recoils from abnormal impurity no more than from normal, and the climax of the book is her full indulgence in both.

Now here we have a specimen of love raised to intensity, but divested as far as possible of the religious element. I say divested as far as possible, because even here, as I shall prove hereafter, the process is not complete, and something of religion is still left fermenting. But it is quite complete enough for our present purpose. It will remind us in the sharpest and clearest way that love is no force which is naturally constant in its development, or which if left to itself can be in any way a moral director to us. It will show us that many of its developments are what the moralist calls abominable, and that the very worst of these may perhaps be the most attractive, and be deliberately presented to us as such by men of the most elaborate culture. We shall thus see that love as a test of conduct, as an aim of life, or as an object of any heroic devotion, is not love in general, but love of a special kind, and that to fulfil this function it must not only be selected from the rest, but also removed from them, and set above them at a quite incalculable distance. And the kind thus chosen, let me repeat again (for this, though less obvious, is more important still), is not chosen because it is naturally intense, but it becomes intense because it is the chosen one.

Here then lies the weak point in the position of the positive moralists, when they hold up such love to us as so supreme a treasure in life. They observe, and quite correctly, that it is looked upon as a treasure; but the source of its preciousness is something that their system expressly takes from it. That choice amongst the loves, so solemn and so imperious and yet so tender, which descends like a tongue of flame upon the love it delights to honour; which fixes on a despised and a weak affection, taking it like Elisha from his furrows, or like David from his pastures, setting it above all its fellows, and making it at once a queen and prophetess—this is a choice that positivism has no power to make; or which, if it makes, it makes only a caprice, or a listless preference. It does not, indeed, confound pure love with impure, but it sets them on an equal footing; and those who contend that the former under these conditions is intrinsically more attractive to men than the latter, betray a most naïve ignorance of what human nature is. Supposing, for argument's sake, that to themselves it may be so, this fact is not of the slightest use to them. It is merely the possession on their part of a certain personal taste, which those who do not share it may regard as disease or weakness, and which they themselves can neither defend nor inculcate. It is true they may call their opponents hard names if they choose; but their opponents can call them hard names back again; but in the absence of any common standard, the recriminations on neither side can have the least sting in them. Could, however, any argument on such a matter be possible, it is the devotees of impurity that would have the strongest case; for the pleasures of indulgence are admitted by both sides, while the merits of abstention are admitted by only one.

Let us go back, for instance, in connection with this matter, to what Professor Huxley has told us is the grand result of education. It leads us away, he says, from 'the rank and steaming valleys of sense,' up to the 'highest good,' which is 'discerned by reason,' 'resting in eternal calm.' And let us ask him again, what, as uttered by a positivist, these words can by any possibility mean. 'The rank and steaming valleys of sense'! Why are they rank and steaming? Or, if they are, why is that any condemnation of them? Or, if we do condemn them, what else are we to praise? The entire raw material, not of our pleasures only, but of our knowledge also, is given us, say the positive school, by the senses. Surely then to condemn the senses must be to condemn life. Let us imagine Professor Huxley talking in this way to Théophile Gautier. Let us imagine him frowning grimly at the licentious Frenchman, and urging him with all vehemence to turn to the highest good. The answer will at once be, 'That is exactly, my dear Professor, what I do turn to. And, listen,' he might say—the following is again a passage from his own writings—'to the way in which I figure the highest good to myself. It is a huge building, with its outer walls all blind and windowless; a huge court within, surrounded by a colonnade of white marble; in the midst a musical fountain with a jet of quick-silver in the Arabian fashion; leaves of orange-trees and pomegranates placed alternately; overhead the bluest of skies and the mellowest of suns; great long-nosed greyhounds should be sleeping here and there; from time to time barefoot negresses with golden ankle-rings, fair women servants white and slender, and clad in rich strange garments, should pass between the hollow arches, basket on arm, or urn poised on head.[19] Three things give me pleasure, gold, marble, and purple—brilliance, mass, and colour. These are the stuffs out of which my dreams are made; and all my ideal palaces are constructed of these materials.'[20] What answer could Professor Huxley make to this that would not seem to the other at once barbarous and nonsensical? The best answer he could make would be simply, 'I do not agree with you.' And to this again the answer would at once be, 'That is because you are still hampered by prejudices, whose only possible foundations we have both removed; and because I am a man of culture, and you are not.'

Let us also consider again that other utterance of Professor Huxley's, with which I began this chapter. According to the positive view of morals, he says, those special sets of happiness that a moral system selects for us, have no more to do with any theory as to the reason of their selection, than a man's sight has to do with his theory of vision, or than the hot taste of ginger has to do with a knowledge of its analysis. That is a most clear and succinct statement of the whole positive position; and we shall now be able to profit by its clearness, and to see how all that it does is to reveal confusion. In the first place, Professor Huxley's comparisons really illustrate the very fact that he designs them to invalidate. It is precisely on his theory of vision that a man's sight practically does depend. All sight, so far as it conveys any meaning to him, is an act of inference; and though generally this process may be so rapid that it is not perceived by him, yet the doubt often felt about distant or unusual objects will make him keenly conscious of it. Whilst as to ginger and the taste produced by it, the moral question is not whether it is hot or not; but whether or no it will be for our advantage to eat it; and this resolves itself into two further questions; firstly, whether its heat is pleasant, and secondly whether its heat is wholesome. On the first of these Professor Huxley throws no light whatever; whilst as to the second, it really hangs entirely on the very point that he cited as indifferent. We must have some knowledge, even though it be only vague and negative, of the nature of a food, before we know whether it will be well for us in the long run to habitually eat it, or to abstain from it.

Let us apply this illustration to love. Professor Huxley's ginger shall stand for the sort of love he would most approve of; and love, as a whole, will be represented by a varied dessert, of which ginger is one of the dishes. Now what Professor Huxley has to do is to recommend this ginger, and to show that it is divided by an infinite gulf—say from prunes or from Huntley and Palmer's biscuits. But how is he to do this? To say that ginger is hot is to say nothing. To many, that may condemn instead of recommending it: and they will have as much to say for their own tastes if they rejoin that prunes and biscuits are sweet. If he can prove to them that what they choose is unwholesome, and that if they eat it they will be too unwell to say their prayers, then, supposing they want to say their prayers, he will have gained his point. But if he cannot prove that it is unwholesome, or if his friends have no prayers to say, his entire recommendation dwindles to a declaration of his own personal taste. But in this case his whole tone will be different. There will be nothing in it of the moral imperative. He will be only laughed at and not listened to, if he proclaims his own taste in sweetmeats with all the thunders of Sinai. And the choice between the various kinds of love is, on positive principles, only a choice between sweetmeats. It is this, and nothing more, than this, avowedly; and yet the positivists would keep for it the earnest language of the Christian, for whom it is a choice, not between sweetmeats and sweetmeats, but between a confectioner's wafer and the Host.

It may perhaps be urged by some that, according to this view of it, purity is degraded into a bitter something, which we only accept reluctantly, through fear of the consequences of its alternatives. And it is quite true that a fear of the consequences of wrong love is inseparably connected with our sense of the value of right love. But this is a necessity of the case; the quality of the right love is in no way lowered by it, and it will lead us to consider another important point.

It is impossible to hold that one thing is incalculably better than others, without holding also that others are incalculably worse than it. Indeed, the surest test we can give of the praise we bestow on what we choose, is the measure of condemnation we bestow on what we reject. If we maintain that virtuous love constitutes its own heaven, we must also maintain that vicious love constitutes its own hell. If we cannot do the last we certainly cannot do the first. And the positive school can do neither. It can neither elevate one kind of love nor depress the others; and for this reason. The results of love in both cases are, according to their teaching, bounded by our present consciousness; and our present consciousness, divorced from all future expectation, has no room in it for so vast an interval as all moral systems postulate between the right love and the wrong. Indeed, if happiness be the test of right, it cannot, as a general truth, be said that they are practically separable at all. It is notorious that, as far as the present life goes, a man of even the vilest affections may effectually elude all pain from them. Sometimes they may injure his health, it is true; but they need not even do that; and if they do, it necessitates no moral condemnation of them, for many heroic labours would do just the same. Injury to the health, at any rate, is a mere accident; so is also injury to the reputation; and conditions are easily conceivable by which both these dangers would be obviated. The supposed evils of impurity have but a very slight reference to these. They depend, not on any present consciousness, but on the expectations of a future consciousness—a consciousness that will reveal things to us hereafter which we can only augur here.

I do not know them now, but after death
God knows I know the faces I shall see:
Each one a murdered self with last low breath,
'I am thyself; what hast thou done to me?'
'And I, and I thyself!' lo each one saith,
'And thou thyself, to all eternity.'21
Such is the expectation on which the supposed evils of impurity depend. According to positive principles, the expectation will never be fulfilled; the evils therefore exist only in a diseased imagination.

And with the beauty of purity the case is just the same. According to the view which the positivists have adopted, so little counting the cost of it, a pure human affection is a union of two things. It is not a possession only, but a promise; not a sentiment only, but a pre-sentiment; not a taste only, but a foretaste; and the chief sweetness said to be found in the former, is dependent altogether upon the latter. 'Blessed are the pure in heart, for they shall see God,' is the belief which, whether true or false as a fact, is implied in the whole modern cultus of love, and the religious reverence with which it has come to be regarded. In no other way can we explain either its eclecticism or its supreme importance. Nor is the belief in question a thing that is implied only. Continually it is expressed also, and this even by writers who theoretically repudiate it. Goethe, for instance, cannot present the moral aspects of Margaret's love-story without assuming it. And George Eliot has been obliged to presuppose it in her characters, and to exhibit the virtues she regards as noblest, on the pedestal of a belief that she regards as most irrational. But its completest expression is naturally to be found elsewhere. Here, for instance, is a verse of Mr. Robert Browning's, [126]who, however we rank him otherwise, is perhaps unrivalled for his subtle analysis of the emotions:

Dear, when our one soul understands
The great soul that makes all things new,
When earth breaks up, and heaven expands,
How will the change strike me and you,
In the house not made with hands?

Here, again, is another, in which the same sentiment is presented in a somewhat different form:

Is there nought better than to enjoy?
No deed which done, will make time break,
Letting us pent-up creatures through
Into eternity, our due—
No forcing earth teach heaven's employ?
No wise beginning, here and now,
Which cannot grow complete (earth's feat)
And heaven must finish there and then?
No tasting earth's true food for men,
Its sweet in sad, its sad in sweet?

To the last of these verses a singular parallel may be found in the works of a much earlier, and a very different writer, only the affection there dealt with is filial and not marital. In spite of this difference, however, it will still be much in point.

'The day was fast approaching,' says Augustine, 'whereon my mother was to depart this life, when it happened, Lord, as I believe by thy special ordinance, that she and I were alone together, leaning in a certain window that[127] looked into the garden of the house, where we were then staying at Ostia. We were talking together alone, very sweetly, and were wondering what the life would be of God's saints in heaven. And when our discourse was come to that point, that the highest delight and brightest of all the carnal senses seemed not fit to be so much as named with that life's sweetness, we, lifting ourselves yet more ardently to the Unchanging One, did by degrees pass through all things bodily—beyond the heaven even, and the sun and stars. Yea, we soared higher yet by inward musing. We came to our own minds, and we passed beyond them, that we might reach that place of plenty, where Thou feedest Israel for ever with the food of truth, and where life is the Wisdom by which all these things are made. And whilst we were discoursing and panting after her, we slightly touched on her with the whole effort of our heart; and we sighed, and there left bound the first fruits of the spirit, and came back again to the sounds of our own mouths—to our own finite language. And what we then said was in this wise: If to any the tumult of the flesh were hushed, hushed the images of the earth and air and waters, hushed too the poles of heaven, yea the very soul be hushed to herself, and by not thinking on self transcend self, hushed all dreams and imaginary revelations, every tongue and every sign, and whatever exists only in transition—if these should all be hushed, having only roused our ears to Him that made them, and He speak alone, not by them but by Himself, that we might hear His word, not through any tongue of flesh, nor angel's voice, nor sound of thunder,[128] nor in the dark riddle of a similitude, but might hear Him, whom in these things we love—His very self without any aid from these (even as we two for that brief moment had touched the eternal Wisdom)—could this be continued on, and other visions, far unlike it, be withdrawn, and this one ravish and absorb and wrap up its beholders amid these inward joys, so that life might be for ever like that one moment of understanding, were not this, Enter thou into the joy of thy Lord? And when shall that be? Shall it be when we rise again, but shall not all be changed?'[22]

In this exceedingly striking passage we have the whole case before us. The belief on which modern love rests, and which makes it so single and so sacred is, as it were, drawn for us on an enlarged scale: and we see that it is a belief to which positivism has no right. The belief, indeed, is by no means a modern thing. Rudiments of it on the contrary are as old as man himself, and may represent a something that inheres in his very nature. But none the more for this will it be of any service to the positivist; for this something can only be of power or value if the prophecy it inevitably develops into be regarded as a true one. In the consciousness of the ancient world it lay undeciphered like the dark sentence of an oracle; and though it might be revered [129]by some, it could not be denied by any. But its meaning is now translated for us, and there is a new factor in the case. We now can deny it; and if we do, its whole power is paralysed.

This when once recognised must be evident enough. But a curious confusion of thought has prevented the positive school from seeing it. They have imagined that what religion adds to love is the hope of prolongation only, not of development also; and thus we find Professor Huxley curtly dismissing the question by saying that the quality of such a pleasure 'is obviously in no way affected by the abbreviation or prolongation of our conscious life.' How utterly this is beside the point may be shown instantly by a very simple example. A painter, we will say, inspired with some great conception, sets to work at a picture, and finds a week of the intensest happiness in preparing his canvas and laying his first colours. Now the happiness of that week is, of course, a fact for him. It would not have been greater had it lasted a whole fortnight; and it would not have been less had he died at the week's end. But though obviously, as Professor Huxley says, it in no way depends on its prolongation, what it does depend on is the belief that it will be prolonged, and that in being prolonged it will change its character. It depends on the belief on the painter's part that he will be able to continue his painting, and that as he continues it, his picture will advance to completion. The positivists have confused the true saying that the pleasure of painting one picture does not depend on the fact that we shall paint many, with the false saying that the pleasure of beginning that one does not depend on the belief that we shall finish it. On this last belief it is plain that the pleasure does depend, largely if not entirely; and it is precisely this last belief that positivism takes away.

To return again, then, to the subject of human love—we are now in a position to see that, as offered us at present by the positive school of moralists, it cannot, properly speaking, be called a positive pleasure at all, but that, it is still essentially a religious one; and that when the religious element is eradicated, its entire character will change. It may be, of course, contended that the religious element is ineradicable: but this is simply either to call positivism an impossibility, or religion an incurable disease. Here, however, we are touching on a side issue, which I shall by and by return to, but which is at present beside the point. My aim now is not to argue either that positivism can or cannot be accepted by humanity, but to show what, if accepted, it will have to offer us. I wish to point out the error, for instance, of such writers as George Eliot, who, whilst denying the existence of any sun-god in the heavens, are yet perpetually adoring the sunlight on the earth; who profess to extinguish all fire on principle, and then offer us boiling water to supply its place; or who, sending love to us as a mere Cassandra, continue to quote as Scripture the prophecies they have just discredited.

Thus far what we have seen is this. Love as a positive pleasure, if it be ever reduced to such, will be a very different thing from what our positivist moralists at present see it to be. It will perform none of those functions for which they now look to it. It will no longer supply them, as now, with any special pinnacle on which human life may raise itself. The one type of it that is at present on an eminence will sink to the same level as the others. All these will be offered to us indiscriminately, and our choice between them will have no moral value. None of the ethical epithets by which these varieties are at present so sharply distinguished from each other will have any virtue left in them. Morality in this connection will be a word without a meaning.

I have as yet dealt only with one of those resources, which have been supposed to impart to life a positive general value. This one, however, has been the most important and the most comprehensive of all; and its case will explain that of the others, and perhaps, with but few exceptions, include them. One or two of these others I shall by and by treat separately; but we will first enquire into the results on life of the change we have been considering already.

[15] Mr. A. C. Swinburne.

[16] Mademoiselle de Maupin, pp. 213-222. Ed. Paris. 1875.

[17] Mademoiselle de Maupin, p. 223.

[18] Ibid., p. 225.

[19] Mademoiselle de Maupin, p. 222.

[20] Ibid., p. 211.

[21] Dante Gabriel Rosetti.

[22] Aug. Conf., lib. ix. In the earlier part of the passage the extreme redundancy of the original has been curtailed somewhat. In the rendering here given I have to a great extent followed Dr. Pusey.

Is Life Worth Living? By William Hurrell Mallock

CHAPTER VI.

LIFE AS ITS OWN REWARD.

'If in this life only we have hope—'
What we have now before us is a certain subtraction sum. We have to take from life one of its strongest present elements; and see as well as we can what will then be the remainder. An exact answer we shall, of course, not expect; but we can arrive at an approximate one without much difficulty.

What we have to subtract has been shown in the previous chapter; but it may again be described briefly in the following way. Life in its present state, as we have just seen, is a union of two sets of feelings, and of two kinds of happiness, and is partly the sum of the two, and partly a compromise between them. Its resources, by one classification, are separable into two groups, according as in themselves they chance to repel or please us; and the most obvious measure of happiness would seem to be nothing more than our gain of what is thus pleasant, and our shirking of what is thus painful. But if we examine life as it actually exists about us, we shall see that this classification has been traversed by another. Many things naturally repellent have received a supernatural blessing; many things naturally pleasant have received a supernatural curse; and thus our highest happiness is often composed of pain, and our profoundest misery is nearly always based on pleasure. Accordingly, whereas happiness naturally would seem the test of right, right has come supernaturally to be the test of happiness. And so completely is this notion engrained in the world's consciousness, that in all our deeper views of life, no matter whether we be saints or sinners, right and wrong are the things that first appeal to us, not happiness and misery. A certain supernatural moral judgment, in fact, has become a primary faculty with us, and it mixes with every estimate we form of the world around us.

It is this faculty that positivism, if accepted fully, must either destroy or paralyse; it is this, therefore, that in imagination we must now try to eliminate. To do this—to see what will be left in life to us, without this faculty, we must first see in general, how much is at present dependent on it.

This might at first sight seem a hard task to perform; the interests we shall have to deal with are so many and so various. But the difficulty may be eluded. I have already gone to literature for examples of special feelings on the part of individuals, and under certain circumstances. We will now go to it for a kindred, though not for the same assistance; and for this end we shall approach it in a slightly different way. What we did before was this. We took certain works of literary art, and selecting, as it were, one or two special patches of colour, we analysed the composition of these. What we shall now do will be to take the pictures as organic wholes, with a view to analysing the effect of them as pictures—the harmony or the contrast of their colours, and the massing of their lights and shadows. If we reflect for a moment what art is—literary and poetical art in particular—we shall at once see how, examined in this way, it will be of use to us. In the first place, then, what is art? and what is the reason that it pleases us? It is a reflection, a reproduction of the pleasures of life, and is altogether relative to these, and dependent on them. We should, for instance, take no interest in portraits unless we took some interest in the human face. We should take none in statues if we took none in the human form. We must know something of love as a feeling, or we should never care for love-songs. Art may send us back to these with intenser appreciation of them, but we must bring to art from life the appreciation we want intensified. Art is a factor in common human happiness, because by its means common men are made partakers in the vision of uncommon men.

135Great art is a speculum reflecting life as the keenest eyes have seen it. All its forms and imagery are of value only as this. Taken by themselves, 'the best in this kind are but shadows.' We have to 'piece out their imperfections, with our thoughts;' 'imagination has to amend them,' and 'it must be our imagination, not theirs.'23 In examining a work of art, then, we are examining life itself; or rather, in examining the interest which we take in a work of art, in examining the reasons why we think it beautiful, or great, or interesting, we are examining our own feelings as to the realities represented by it.

And now remembering this, let us turn to certain of the world's greatest works of art—I mean its dramas: for just as poetry is the most articulate of all the arts, so is the drama the most comprehensive form of poetry. In the drama we have the very thing we are now in want of. We have life as a whole—that complex aggregate of details, which forms, as it were, the mental landscape of existence, presented to us in a 'questionable shape,' at once concentrated and intensified. And it is no exaggeration to say that the reasons why men think life worth 136living, can be all found in the reasons why they think a great drama great.

Let us turn, then, to some of the greatest works of Sophocles, of Shakespeare, and of Goethe, and consider briefly how these present life to us. Let us take Macbeth, Hamlet, Measure for Measure, and Faust. We have here five presentations of life, under what confessedly are its most striking aspects, and with such interests as men have been able to find in it, raised to their greatest intensity. Such, at least, is the way in which these works are regarded, and it is only in virtue of this estimate that they are called great. Now, in producing this estimate, what is the chief faculty in us that they appeal to? It will need but little thought to show us that they appeal primarily to the supernatural moral judgment; that this judgment is perpetually being expressed explicitly in the works themselves; and, which is far more important, that it is always pre-supposed in us. In other words, these supreme presentations of life are presentations of men struggling, or failing to struggle, not after natural happiness, but after supernatural right; and it is always pre-supposed on our part that we admit this struggle to be the one important thing. And this importance, we shall see further, is based, not on the external and the social consequences of conduct, but essentially and primarily on its internal and its personal consequences.

In Macbeth, for instance, the main incident, the tragic-colouring matter of the drama, is the murder of Duncan. But in what aspect of this does the real tragedy lie? Not in the fact that Duncan is murdered, but in the fact that Macbeth is the murderer. What appals us, what purges our passions with pity and with terror as we contemplate it, is not the external, the social effect of the act, but the personal, the internal effect of it. As for Duncan, he is in his grave; after life's fitful fever he sleeps well. What our minds are made to dwell upon is not that Duncan shall sleep for ever, but that Macbeth shall sleep no more; it is not the extinction of a dynasty, but the ruin of a character.

We see in Hamlet precisely the same thing. The action there that our interest centres in, is the hero's struggle to conform to an internal personal standard of right, utterly irrespective of use to others, or of natural happiness to himself. In the course of this struggle, indeed, he does nothing but ruin the happiness around him; and this ruin adds greatly to the pathos of the spectacle. But we are not indignant with Hamlet, as being the cause of it. We should have been indignant rather with him if the case had been reversed, and if, instead of sacrificing social happiness for the sake of personal right, he had sacrificed personal right for the sake of social happiness.

In Antigone the case is just the same, only there its nature is yet more distinctly exhibited. We have for the central interest the same personal struggle after right, not after use or happiness; and one of the finest passages in that whole marvellous drama is a distinct statement by the heroine that this is so. The one rule she says, that she is resolved to live by, and not live by only, but if needs be to die for, is no human rule, is no standard of man's devising, nor can it be modified to suit our changing needs; but it is

The unwritten and the enduring laws of God,
Which are not of to-day nor yesterday,
But live from everlasting, and none breathes
Who knows them, whence begotten.

In Measure for Measure and Faust we can see the matter reduced to a narrower issue still. In both these plays we can see at once that one moral judgment at least, not to name others, is before all things pre-supposed in us. This is a hard and fixed judgment with regard to female chastity, and the supernatural value of it. It is only because we assent to this judgment that Isabella is heroic to us; and primarily for the same reason that Margaret is unfortunate. Let us suspend this judgment for a moment, and what will become of these two dramas? The terror and the pity of them will vanish instantly like a dream. The fittest name for both of them will be 'Much Ado about Nothing.'

It will thus be seen, and the more we consider the matter the more plain will it become to us—that in all such art as that which we have been now considering, the premiss on which all its power and greatness rests is this: The grand relation of man is not first to his brother men, but to something else, that is beyond humanity—that is at once without and also beyond himself; to this first, and to his brother men through this. We are not our own; we are bought with a price. Our bodies are God's temples, and the joy and the terror of life depends on our keeping these temples pure, or defiling them. Such are the solemn and profound beliefs, whether conscious or unconscious, on which all the higher art of the world has based itself. All the profundity and solemnity of it is borrowed from these, and exists for us in exact proportion to the intensity with which we hold them.

Nor is this true of sublime and serious art only. It is true of cynical, profligate, and concupiscent art as well. It is true of Congreve as it is true of Sophocles; it is true of Mademoiselle de Maupin as it is true of Measure for Measure. This art differs from the former in that the end presented in it as the object of struggle is not only not the morally right, but is also to a certain extent essentially the morally wrong. In the case of cynical and profligate art this is obvious. For such art does not so much depend on the substitution of some new object, as in putting insult on the present one. It does not make right and wrong change places; on the contrary it carefully keeps them where they are; but it insults the former by transferring its insignia to the latter. It is not the ignoring of the right, but the denial of it. Cynicism and profligacy are essentially the spirits that deny, but they must retain the existing affirmations for their denial to prey upon. Their function is not to destroy the good, but to keep it in lingering torture. It is a kind of spiritual bear-baiting. They hate the good, and its existence piques them; but they must know that the good exists none the less. 'I'd no sooner,' says one of Congreve's characters, 'play with a man that slighted his ill-fortune, than I'd make love to a woman who undervalued the loss of her reputation.' In this one sentence is contained the whole secret of profligacy; and profligacy is the same as cynicism, only it is cynicism sensualized. Now we have in the above sentence the exact counterpart to the words of Antigone that I have already quoted. For just as her life lay in conformity to 'The unwritten, and the enduring laws of God,' so does the life of the profligate lie in the violation of them. To each the existence of laws is equally essential. For profligacy is not merely the gratification of the appetites, but the gratification of them at the expense of something else. Beasts are not profligate. We cannot have a profligate goat.

In what I have called concupiscent art, the case might seem different, and to a certain extent it is so. The objects of struggle that we are there presented with are meant to be presented as pleasures, not in defiance of right and wrong, but independently of them. The chief of these, indeed, as Théophile Gautier has told us, are the physical endearments of a man and a woman, with no other qualification than that they are both of them young and beautiful. But though this art professes to be thus independent of the moral judgment, and to trust for none of its effects to the discernment between good and evil, this really is very far from being the case. Let us turn once again to the romance we have already quoted from. The hero says, as we have seen already, that he has completely lost the power of discernment in question. Now, even this, as might be shown easily, is not entirely true; for argument's sake, however, we may grant him that it is so. The real point in the matter to notice is that he is at any rate conscious of the loss. He is a man tingling with the excitement of having cast off some burden. The burden may be gone, but it is still present in the sharp effects of its absence. He is a kind of moral poacher, who, though he may not live by law, takes much of his life's tone from the sense that he is eluding it. His pleasures, though pleasurable in themselves, yet have this quality heightened by the sense of contrast. 'I am at any rate not virtuous,' his mistress says to him, 'and that is always something gained.' George Eliot says of Maggie Tulliver, that she liked her aunt Pullet chiefly because she was not her aunt Gleg. Théophile Gautier's hero likes the Venus Anadyomene, partly at least, because she is not the Madonna.

Nay, let us even descend to worse spectacles—to the sight of men struggling for enjoyments that are yet more obviously material, more devoid yet of any trace of mind or morals, and we shall see plainly, if we consult the mirror of art, that the moral element is present even here. We shall trace it even in such abnormal literature of indulgence as the erotic work commonly ascribed to Meursius. We shall trace it in the orgies of Tiberius at Capri; or of Quartilla, as Petronius describes them, at Neapolis. It is like a ray of light coming in at the top of a dark cavern, whose inmates see not it, but by it; and which only brings to them a consciousness of shadow. It is this supernatural element that leavens natural passion, and gives its mad rage to it. It creates for it 'a twilight where virtues are vices.' The pleasures thus sought for are supposed to enthral men not in proportion to their intensity (for this through all their varieties would be probably nearly equal) but in proportion to their lowness—to their sullying power. Degradation is the measure of enjoyment; or rather it is an increasing numeral by which one constant figure of enjoyment is multiplied.

Ah, where shall we go then, for pastime,

If the worst that can be has been done?
This is the great question of the votaries of such joys as these.24

Thus if we look at life in the mirror of art, we shall see how the supernatural is ever present to us. If we climb up into heaven it is there; if we go down into hell it is there also. We shall see it at the bottom of those two opposite sets of pleasures, to the one or the other of which all human pleasures belong. The source of one is an impassioned struggle after the supernatural right, or an impassioned sense of rest upon attaining it; the source of the other is the sense of revolt against it, which in various ways flatters or excites us. In both cases the supernatural moral judgment is the sense appealed to, primarily in the first case, and secondarily if not primarily in the second. All the life about us is coloured by this, and naturally if this be destroyed or wrecked, the whole aspect of life will change for us. What then will this change be? Looking still into the mirror of art, the general character of it will 144be very readily perceptible. I noticed just now, in passing, how Measure for Measure and Faust would suffer in their meaning and their interest, by the absence on our part of a certain moral judgment. They would become like a person singing to a deaf audience—a series of dumb grimaces with no meaning in them. The same thing is equally true in all the other cases. Antigone's heroism will evaporate;25 she will be left obstinate only. The lives of Macbeth and Hamlet will be tales of little meaning for us, though the words are strong. They will be full of sound and fury, but they will signify nothing. What they produce in us will be not interest but a kind of wondering weariness—weariness at the weary fate of men who could 'think so brainsickly of things.' So in like manner will all the emphasis and elaboration in the literature of sensuality become a weariness without meaning, also. Congreve's caustic wit will turn to spasmodic truism; and Théophile Gautier's excess of erotic ardour, into prolix and fantastic affectation. All its sublimity, its brilliance, and a large part of its interest, depend in art on the existence of the moral sense, and would in its absence be absolutely unproducible. The reason of this is plain. The natural pains and pleasures of 145life, merely manipulated by the imagination and the memory, have too little variety or magnitude in them without further aid. Art without the moral sense to play upon, is like a pianist whose keyboard is reduced to a single octave.

And exactly the same will be the case with life. Life will lose just the same qualities that art will—neither more nor less. There will be no introduction of any new interests, but merely the elimination of certain existing ones. The subtraction of the moral sense will not revolutionise human purposes, but simply make them listless. It will reduce to a parti-coloured level the whole field of pains and pleasures. The moral element gives this level a new dimension. Working underneath it as a subterranean force, it convulses and divides its surface. Here vast areas subside into valleys and deep abysses; there mountain peaks shoot up heavenwards. Mysterious shadows begin to throng the hollows; new tints and half-tints flicker and shift everywhere; mists hang floating over ravines and precipices; the vegetation grows more various, here slenderer, there richer and more luxuriant; whilst high over all, bright on the topmost summits, is a new strange something—the white snows of purity, catching the morning streaks on them of a brighter day, that has never as yet risen upon the world below.

With the subtraction, or nullifying, of the moral force, all this will go. The mountains will sink, the valleys be filled up; all will be once more dead level—still indeed parti-coloured, but without light and shadow, and with the colours reduced in number, and robbed of all their vividness. The chiaro-oscuro will have gone from life; the moral landscape, whose beauty and grandeur is at present so much extolled, will have dissolved like an insubstantial pageant. Vice and virtue will be set before us in the same grey light; every deeper feeling either of joy or sorrow, of desire or of repulsion, will lose its vigour, and cease any more to be resonant.

It may be said indeed, and very truly, that under favourable circumstances there must always remain a joy in the mere act of living, in the exercising of the bodily functions, and in the exciting and appeasing of the bodily appetites. Will anything, it may be asked, for instance, rob the sunshine of its gladness, or deaden the vital influence of a spring morning?—when the sky is a cloudless blue, and the sea is like a wild hyacinth, when the pouring brooks seem to live as they sparkle, and the early air amongst the woodlands has the breath in it of unseen violets? All this, it is quite true, will be left to us; this and a great deal more. This, however, is but one side of the picture. If life has its own natural gladness which is expressed by spring, it has also its own natural sadness which is expressed by winter; and the worth of life, if this is all we trust to, will be as various and as changing as the weather is. But this is not all. Even this worth, such as it is, depends for us at present, in a large measure, upon religion—not directly indeed, but indirectly. This life of air, and nerve, and muscle, this buoyant consciousness of joyous and abounding health, which seems so little to have connection with faiths or theories, is for us impregnated with a life that is impregnated with these, and thus their subtle influence pervades it everywhere. There is no impulse from without which stirs or excites the senses, that does not either bring to us, or send us on to, a something beyond itself. In each of these pleasures that seems to us so simple, floats a swarm of hopes and memories, like the gnats in a summer twilight. There is not a sight, a sound, a smell, not a breath from sea or garden, that is not full of them, and on which, busy and numberless, they are not wafted into us. And each of these volatile presences brings the notions of right and wrong with it; and it is these that make sensuous life tingle with so strange and so elaborate an excitement. Indirectly then, though not directly, the mere joy in the act of living will suffer from the loss of religion, in the same manner, though perhaps not in the same degree, as the other joys will. It will not lose its existence, but it will lose zest. The fabric of its pleasures will of course remain what it ever was; but its brightest inhabitants will have left it. It will be as desolate as Mayfair in September, or as a deserted college during a long vacation.

We may here pause in passing, to remark on the shallowness of that philosophy of culture, to be met with in certain quarters, which, whilst admitting all that can be said as to the destruction for us of any moral obligation, yet advises us still to profit by the variety of moral distinctions. 'Each moment,' says Mr. Pater for instance, 'some form grows perfect in hand or face; some tone on the hills or sea is choicer than the rest; some mood of passion or insight or intellectual excitement, is irresistibly real and attractive for us.' And thus, he adds, 'while all melts under our feet, we may well catch at any exquisite passion, or any contribution to knowledge, that seems by a lifted horizon to set the spirit free for a moment, or any stirring of the senses, strange dyes, strange flowers, and curious odours, or the work of the artist's hand, or the face of one's friend.' It is plain that this positive teaching of culture is open to the same objections, and is based on the same fallacy, as the positive teaching of morals. It does not teach us, indeed, to let right and wrong guide us in the choice of our pleasures, in the sense that we should choose the one sort and eschew the other; but teaching us to choose the two, in one sense indifferently, it yet teaches us to choose them as distinct and contrasted things. It teaches us in fact to combine the two fruits without confusing their flavours. But in the case of good and evil, as has been seen, this is quite impossible; for good is only good as the thing that ought to be chosen; evil is only evil as the thing that ought not to be chosen; and the only reasons that could justify us in combining them would altogether prevent our distinguishing them. The teachings of positive culture, in fact, rest on the naïve supposition that shine and shadow, as it were, are portable things; and that we can take bright objects out of the sunshine, and dark objects out of the shadow, and setting them both together in the diffused grey light of a studio, make a magical mosaic out of them, of gloom and glitter. Or such teachings, to put the matter yet more simply, are like telling us to pick a primrose at noonday, and to set it by our bed-side for a night-light.

It is plain therefore that, in that loss of zest and interest, which the deadening of the moral sense, as we have seen, must bring to life, we shall get no help there. The massy fabric of which saints and heroes were the builders, will never be re-elected by this mincing moral dandyism.

But there is another last resource of the modern school, which is far more worthy of attention, and which, being entirely sui generis, I have reserved to treat of here. That resource is the devotion to truth as truth; not for the sake of its consequences, but in scorn of them. Here we are told we have at least one moral end that can never be taken away from us. It will still survive to give life a meaning, a dignity, and a value, even should the pursuit of it prove destructive to all the others. The language used by the modern school upon this subject is very curious and instructive. I will take two typical instances. The common argument, says Dr. Tyndall, in favour of belief is the comfort and the gladness that it brings us, its redemption of life, in fact, from that dead and dull condition we have been just considering. 'To this,' he says, 'my reply is that I choose the nobler part of Emerson when, after various disenchantments, he exclaimed "I covet truth!" The gladness of true heroism, visits the heart of him who is really competent to say this.' The following sentences are Professor Huxley's: 'If it is demonstrated to me,' he says, 'that without this or that theological dogma the human race will lapse into bipedal cattle, more brutal than the beasts by reason of their greater cleverness, my next question is to ask for the proof of the dogma. If this proof is forthcoming, it is my conviction that no drowning sailor ever clutched a hen-coop more tenaciously than mankind will hold by such dogma, whatever it may be. But if not, then I verily believe that the human race will go its own evil way; and my only consolation lies in the reflection that, however bad our posterity may become, so long as they hold by the plain rule of not pretending to believe what they have no reason to believe, because it may be to their advantage so to pretend, they will not have reached the lowest depths of immorality.' I will content myself with these two instances, but others of a similar kind might be multiplied indefinitely.

Now by a simple substitution of terms, such language as this will reveal at once one important fact to us. According to the avowed principles of positive morality, morality has no other test but happiness. Immorality, therefore, can have no conceivable meaning but unhappiness, or at least the means to it, which in this case are hardly distinguishable from the end; and thus, according to the above rigid reasoners, the human race will not have reached the lowest depths of misery so long as it rejects the one thing which ex hypothesi might render it less miserable. Either then all this talk about truth must really be so much irrelevant nonsense, or else, if it be not nonsense, the test of conduct is something distinct from happiness. The question before us is a plain one, which may be answered in one of two ways, but which positivism cannot possibly answer in both. Is truth to be sought only because it conduces to happiness, or is happiness only to be sought for when it is based on truth? In the latter case truth, not happiness, is the test of conduct. Are our positive moralists prepared to admit this? If so, let them explicitly and consistently say so. Let them keep this test and reject the other, for the two cannot be fused together.

οξος τ' αλειφα τ' εγχεας ταυτω κυτει
διχοστατουντ αν ου φιλοιν προσεννεποις.

This inconsistency is here, however, only a side point—a passing illustration of the slovenliness of the positivist logic. As far as my present argument goes, we may let this pass altogether, and allow the joint existence of these mutually exclusive ends. What I am about to do is to show that on positive grounds the last of these is more hopelessly inadequate than the first—that truth as a moral end has even more of religion in its composition than happiness, and that when this religion goes, its value will even more hopelessly evaporate.

At first sight this may seem impossible. The devotion to truth may seem as simple as it is sacred. But if we consider the matter further, we shall soon think differently. To begin then; truth, as the positivists speak of it, is plainly a thing that is to be worshipped in two ways—firstly by its discovery, and secondly by its publication. Thus Professor Huxley, however much it may pain him, will not hide from himself the fact that there is no God; and however bad this knowledge may be for humanity, his highest and most sacred duty still consists in imparting it. Now why should this be? I ask. Is it simply because the fact in question is the truth? That surely cannot be so, as a few other examples will show us. A man discovers that his wife has been seduced by his best friend. Is there anything very high or very sacred in that discovery? Having made it, does he feel any consolation in the knowledge that it is the entire truth? And will the 'gladness of true heroism' visit him if he proclaims it to everyone in his club? A chattering nurse betrays his danger to a sick man. The sick man takes fright and dies. Was the discovery of the truth of his danger very glorious for the patient? or was its publication very sacred in the nurse? Clearly the truths that it is sacred to find out and to publish are not all truths, but truths of a certain kind only. They are not particular truths like these, but the universal and eternal truths that underlie them. They are in fact what we call the truths of Nature, and the apprehension of them, or truth as attained by us, means the putting ourselves en rapport with the life of that infinite existence which surrounds and sustains all of us. Now since it is this kind of truth only that is supposed to be so sacred, it is clear that its sacredness does not depend on itself, but on its object. Truth is sacred because Nature is sacred; Nature is not sacred because truth is; and our supreme duty to truth means neither more nor less than a supreme faith in Nature. It means that there is a something in the Infinite outside ourselves that corresponds to a certain something within ourselves; that this latter something is the strongest and the highest part of us, and that it can find no rest but in communion with its larger counterpart. Truth sought for in this way is evidently a distinct thing from the truth of utilitarianism. It is no false reflection of human happiness in the clouds. For it is to be sought for none the less, as our positivists decidedly tell us, even though all other happiness should be ruined by it. Now what on positive principles is the groundwork of this teaching? All ethical epithets such as sacred, heroic, and so forth—all the words, in fact, that are by implication applied to Nature—have absolutely no meaning save as applied to conscious beings; and as a subject for positive observation, there exists no consciousness in the universe outside this earth. By what conceivable means, then, can the positivists transfer to Nature in general qualities which, so far as they know, are peculiar to human nature only? They can only do this in one of two ways—both of which they would equally repudiate—either by an act of fancy, or by an act of faith. Tested rigidly by their own fundamental common principles, it is as unmeaning to call the universe sacred as to say that the moon talks French.

Let us however pass this by; let us refuse to subject their teaching to the extreme rigour of even their own law; and let us grant that by some mixed use of fancy or of mysticism, they can turn to Nature as to some vast moral hieroglyph. What sort of morality do they find in it? Nature, as positive observation reveals her to us, is a thing that can have no claim either on our reverence or our approbation. Once apply any moral test to her conduct, and as J. S. Mill has so forcibly pointed out, she becomes a monster. There is no crime that men abhor or perpetrate that Nature does not commit daily on an exaggerated scale. She knows no sense either of justice or mercy. Continually indeed she seems to be tender, and loving, and bountiful; but all that, at such times, those that know her can exclaim to her, is

Miseri quibus
Intentata nites.

At one moment she will be blessing a country with plenty, peace, and sunshine; and she will the next moment ruin the whole of it by an earthquake. Now she is the image of thrift, now of prodigality; now of the utmost purity, now of the most revolting filth; and if, as I say, she is to be judged by any moral standard at all, her capacities for what is admirable not only make her crimes the darker, but they also make her virtues partake of the nature of sin. How, then, can an intimacy with this eternal criminal be an ennobling or a sacred thing? The theist, of course, believes that truth is sacred. But his belief rests on a foundation that has been altogether renounced by the positivists. He values truth because, in whatever direction it takes him, it takes him either to God or towards Him—God, to whom he is in some sort akin, and after whose likeness he is in some sort made. He sees Nature to be cruel, wicked, and bewildering when viewed by itself. But behind Nature he sees a vaster power—his father—in whom mysteriously all contradictions are reconciled. Nature for him is God's, but it is not God; and 'though God slay me,' he says, 'yet will I trust in Him.' This trust can be attained to only by an act of faith like this. No observation or experiment, or any positive method of any kind, will be enough to give it us; rather, without faith, observation and experiment will do nothing but make it seem impossible. Thus a belief in the sacredness of Nature, or, in other words, in the essential value of truth, is as strictly an act of religion, as strictly a defiance of the whole positive formula, as any article in any ecclesiastical creed. It is simply a concrete form of the beginning of the Christian symbol, 'I believe in God the Father Almighty.' It rests on the same foundation, neither more nor less. Nor is it too much to say that without a religion, without a belief in God, no fetish-worship was ever more ridiculous than this cultus of natural truth.

This subject is so important that it will be well to dwell on it a little longer. I will take another passage from Dr. Tyndall, which presents it to us in a slightly different light, and which speaks explicitly not of truth itself, but of that sacred Object beyond, of which truth is only the sacramental channel to us. '"Two things," said Imanuel Kant' (it is thus Dr. Tyndall writes), '"fill me with awe—the starry heavens, and the sense of moral responsibility in man." And in the hours of health and strength and sanity, when the stroke of action has ceased, and when the pause of reflection has set in, the scientific investigator finds himself overshadowed by the same awe. Breaking contact with the hampering details of earth, it associates him with a power which gives fulness and tone to his existence, but which he can neither analyse nor comprehend.' This, Dr. Tyndall tells us, is the only rational statement of the fact of that 'divine communion,' whose nature is 'simply distorted and desecrated' by the unwarranted assumptions of theism.

Now let us try to consider accurately what Dr. Tyndall's statement means. Knowledge of Nature, he says, associates him with Nature. It withdraws him from 'the hampering details of earth,' and enables the individual human being to have communion with a something that is beyond humanity. But what is communion? It is a word with no meaning at all save as referring to conscious beings. There could be no communion between two corpses; nor, again, between a corpse and a living man. Dr. Tyndall, for instance, could have no communion with a dead canary. Communion implies the existence on both sides of a common something. Now what is there in common between Dr. Tyndall and the starry heavens, or that 'power' of which the starry heavens are the embodiment? Dr. Tyndall expressly says that he not only does not know what there is in common, but that he 'dare' not even say that, as conscious beings, they two have anything in common at all.26 The only things he can know about the power in question are that it is vast, and that it is uniform; but a contemplation of these qualities by themselves, must tend rather to produce in him a sense of separation from it than of union with it. United with it, in one sense, he of course is; he is a fraction of the sum of things, and everything, in a certain way, is dependent upon everything else. But in this union there is nothing special. Its existence is an obvious fact, common to all men, whether they dwell upon it or no: and though by a knowledge of Nature we may grow to realise it more keenly, it is impossible to make the union in the least degree closer, or to turn it into anything that can be in any way called a communion. Indeed, for the positivists to talk about communion or association with Nature is about as rational as to talk about communion or association with a steam-engine. The starry skies at night are doubtless an imposing spectacle; but man, on positive principles, can be no more raised by watching them than a commercial traveller can by watching a duke—probably far less: for if the duke were well behaved, the commercial traveller might perhaps learn some manners from him; but there is nothing in the panorama of the universe that can in any way be any model for the positivist. There are but two respects in which he can compare himself to the rest of nature—firstly, as a revealed force; and, secondly, as a force that works by law. But the forces that are revealed by the stars, for instance, are vast, and the force revealed in himself is small; and he, as he considers, is a self-determining agent, and the stars are not. There are but two points of comparison between the two; and in these two points they are contrasts, and not likenesses. It is true, indeed, as I said just now, that a sense of awe and of hushed solemnity is, as a fact, born in us at the spectacle of the starry heavens—world upon luminous world shining and quivering silently; it is true, too, that a spontaneous feeling connects such a sense somehow with our deepest moral being. But this, on positive principles, must be feeling only. It means absolutely nothing: it can have no objective fact that corresponds to it. It is an illusion, a pathetic fallacy. And to say that the heavens with their stars declare to us anything high or holy, is no more rational than to say that Brighton does, which itself, seen at night from the sea, is a long braid of stars descended upon the wide horizon. All that the study of nature, all that the love of truth, can do for the positivist is not to guide him to any communion with a vaster power, but to show him that no such communion is possible. His devotion to truth, if it mean anything—and the language he often uses about it betrays this—let us know the worst, not let us find out the best:—a wish which is neither more nor less noble than the wish to sit down at once in a slop upon the floor rather than sustain oneself any longer above it on a chair that is discovered to be rickety.

Here then again, in this last resource of positivism we have religion embodied as a yet more important element than in any of the others; and when this element is driven out of it, it collapses yet more hopelessly than they do. By the whole positive system we are bound to human life. There is no mystical machinery by which we can rise above it. It is by its own isolated worth that this life must stand or fall.

And what, let us again ask, will this worth, be? The question is of course, as I have said, too vague to admit of more than a general answer, but a general answer, as I have said also, may be given confidently enough. Man when fully imbued with the positive view of himself, will inevitably be an animal of far fewer capacities than he at present is. He will not be able to suffer so much; but also he will not be able to enjoy so much. Surround him, in imagination, with the most favourable circumstances; let social progress have been carried to the utmost perfection; and let him have access to every happiness of which we can conceive him capable. It is impossible even thus to conceive of life as a very valuable possession to him. It would at any rate be far less valuable than it is to many men now, under outer circumstances that are far less favourable. The goal to which a purely human progress is capable of conducting us, is thus no vague condition of glory and felicity, in which men shall develop new and ampler powers. It is a condition in which, the keenest life attainable has continually been far surpassed already, without anything having been arrived at that in itself seemed of surpassing value.

[23] 'Hippolyta.—This is the silliest stuff I ever heard. Theseus.—The best in this kind are but shadows, and the worst no worse, if imagination amend them. Hippolyta.—It must be your imagination then, not theirs.'—Midsummer's Night's Dream, Act V.

'Piece out our imperfections with your thoughts.'—Prologue to Henry V.

[24] Seneca says of virtue, 'Non quia delectat placet, sed quia placet delectat.' Of vice in the same way we may say, 'Non quia delectat pudet, sed quia pudet delectat.'

[25] It will be of course recollected that in this abstraction of the moral sense, we have to abstract it from the characters as well as ourselves.

[26] 'When I attempt to give the power which I see manifested in the universe an objective form, personal or otherwise, it slips away from me, declining all intellectual manipulation. I dare not, save poetically, use the pronoun "He" regarding it. I dare not call it a "Mind." I refuse even to call it a "Cause." Its mystery overshadows me; but it remains a mystery, while the objective frames which my neighbours try to make it fit, simply distort and desecrate it.'—Dr. Tyndall, 'Materialism and its Opponents.'

Is Life Worth Living? By William Hurrell Mallock

CHAPTER VII.

THE SUPERSTITION OF POSITIVISM.

Glendower. I can call spirits from the vasty deep.
Hotspur. Why so can I, or so can any man,
But will they come when you do call for them?
Henry IV. Part 1.

General and indefinite as the foregoing considerations have been, they are quite definite enough to be of the utmost practical import. They are definite enough to show the utter hollowness of that vague faith in progress, and the glorious prospects that lie before humanity, on which the positive school at present so much rely, and about which so much is said. To a certain extent, indeed, a faith in progress is perfectly rational and well grounded. There are many imperfections in life, which the course of events tends manifestly to lessen if not to do away with, and so far as these are concerned, improvements may go on indefinitely. But the things that this progress touches are, as has been said before, not happiness, but the negative conditions of it. A belief in this kind of progress is not peculiar to positivism. It is common to all educated men, no matter what their creed may be. What is peculiar to positivism is the strange corollary to this belief, that man's subjective powers of happiness will go on expanding likewise. It is the belief not only that the existing pleasures will become more diffused, but that they will, as George Eliot says, become 'more intense in diffusion.' It is this belief on which the positivists rely to create that enthusiasm, that impassioned benevolence, which is to be the motive power of their whole ethical machinery. They have taken away the Christian heaven, and have thus turned adrift a number of hopes and aspirations that were once powerful. These hopes and aspirations they acknowledge to be of the first necessity; they are facts, they say, of human nature, and no higher progress would be possible without them. What the enlightened thought is to do is not to extinguish, but to transfer them. They are to be given a new object more satisfactory than the old one; not our own private glory in another world, but the common glory of our whole race in this.

Now let us consider for a moment some of the positive criticisms on the Christian heaven, and then apply them to the proposed substitute. The belief in heaven, say the positivists, is to be set aside for two great reasons. In the first place there is no objective proof of its existence, and in the second place there is subjective proof of its impossibility. Not only is it not deducible, but it is not even thinkable. Give the imagination carte blanche to construct it, and the imagination will either do nothing, or will do something ridiculous. 'My position [with regard to this matter]' says a popular living writer,27 'is this—The idea of a glorified energy in an ampler life, is an idea utterly incompatible with exact thought, one which evaporates in contradictions, in phrases, which when pressed have no meaning.'

Now if this criticism has the least force, as used against the Christian heaven, it has certainly far more as used against the future glories of humanity. The positivists ask the Christians how they expect to enjoy themselves in heaven. The Christians may, with far more force, ask the positivists how they expect to enjoy themselves on earth. For the Christians' heaven being ex hypothesi an unknown world, they do not stultify their expectations from being unable to describe them. On the contrary it is a part of their faith that they are indescribable. But the positivists' heaven is altogether in this world; and no mystical faith has any place in their system. In this case, therefore, whatever we may think of the other, it is plain that the tests in question are altogether complete and final. To the Christians, indeed, it is quite open to make their supposed shame their glory, and to say that their heaven would be nothing if describable. The positivists have bound themselves to admit that theirs is nothing unless describable.

What then, let us ask the enthusiasts of humanity, will humanity be like in its ideally perfect state? Let them show us some sample of the general future perfection; let them describe one of the nobler, ampler, glorified human beings of the future. What will he be like? What will he long for? What will he take pleasure in? How will he spend his days? How will he make love? What will he laugh at? And let him be described in phrases which when pressed do not evaporate in contradictions, but which have some distinct meaning, and are not incompatible with exact thought. Do our exact thinkers in the least know what they are prophesying? If not, what is the meaning of their prophecy? The prophecies of the positive school are rigid scientific inferences; they are that or nothing. And one cannot infer an event of whose nature one is wholly ignorant.

Let these obvious questions be put to our positive moralists—these questions they have themselves suggested, and the grotesque unreality of this vague optimism will be at once apparent. Never was vagary of mediæval faith so groundless as this. The Earthly Paradise that the mediæval world believed in was not more mythical than the Earthly Paradise believed in by our exact thinkers now; and George Eliot might just as well start in a Cunard steamer to find the one, as send her faith into the future to find the other.

Could it be shown that these splendid anticipations were well founded, they might perhaps kindle some new and active enthusiasm; though it is very doubtful, even then, if the desire would be ardent enough to bring about its own accomplishment. This, however, it is quite useless to consider, the anticipations in question being simply an empty dream. A certain kind of improvement, as I have said, we are no doubt right in looking for, not only with confidence, but with complacency. But positivism, so far from brightening this prospect, makes it indefinitely duller than it would be otherwise. The practical results therefore to be looked for from a faith in progress may be seen at their utmost already in the world around us; and the positivists may make the sobering reflection that their system can only change these from what they already see them, not by strengthening, but by weakening them. Take the world then as it is at present, and the sense, on the individual's part, that he personally is promoting its progress, can belong to, and can stimulate, exceptional men only, who are doing some public work; and it will be found even in these cases that the pleasure which this sense gives them is largely fortified (as is said of wine) by the entirely alien sense of fame and power. On the generality of men it neither has, nor can have, any effect whatever, or even if it gives a glow to their inclinations in some cases, it will at any rate never curb them in any. The fact indeed that things in general do tend to get better in certain ways, must produce in most men not effort but acquiescence. It may, when the imagination brings it home to them, shed a pleasing light occasionally over the surface of their private lives: but it would be as irrational to count on this as a stimulus to farther action, as to expect that the summer sunshine would work a steam-engine.

If we consider, then, that even the present condition of things is far more calculated to produce the enthusiasm of humanity than the condition that the positivists are preparing for themselves, we shall see how utterly chimerical is their entire practical system. It is like a drawing of a cathedral, which looks magnificent at the first glance, but which a second glance shows to be composed of structural impossibilities—blocks of masonry resting on no foundations, columns hanging from the roofs, instead of supporting them, and doors and windows with inverted arches. The positive system could only work practically were human nature to suffer a complete change—a change which it has no spontaneous tendency to make, which no known power could ever tend to force on it, and which, in short, there is no ground of any kind for expecting.

There are two characteristics in men, for instance, which, though they undoubtedly do exist, the positive system requires to be indefinitely magnified—the imagination, and unselfishness. The work of the imagination is to present to the individual consciousness the remote ends to which all progress is to be directed; and the desire to work for these is, on the positive supposition, to conquer all mere personal impulses. Now men have already had an end set before them, in the shape of the joys of heaven, which was far brighter and far more real to them than these others can ever be; and yet the imagination has so failed to keep this before them, that its small effect upon their lives is a commonplace with the positivists themselves. How then can these latter hope that their own pale and distant ideal will have a more vivid effect on the world than that near and glowing one, in whose place they put it? Will it incite men to virtues to which heaven could not incite them? or lure them away from vices from which hell-fire would not scare them? Before it can do so, it is plain that human nature must have completely changed, and its elements have been re-mixed, in completely new proportions. In a state of things where such a result was possible, a man would do a better day's work for a penny to be given to his unborn grandson, than he would now do for a pound to be paid to himself at sunset.

For argument's sake, however, let us suppose such a change possible. Let us suppose the imagination to be so developed that the remote end of progress—that happier state of men in some far off century—is ever vividly present to us as a possibility we may help to realise. Another question still remains for us. To preserve this happiness for others, we are told, we must to a large extent sacrifice our own. Is it in human nature to make this sacrifice? The positive moralists assure us that it is, and for this reason. Man, they say, is an animal who enjoys vicariously with almost as much zest as in his own person; and therefore to procure a greater pleasure for others makes him far happier than to procure a less one for himself. In this statement, as I have observed in an earlier chapter, there is no doubt a certain general truth; but how far it will hold good in particular instances depends altogether on particular circumstances. It depends on the temperament of the person who is to make the sacrifice, on the nature of his feelings towards the person for whom he is to make it, and on the proportion between the pleasure he is to forego himself, and the pleasure he is to secure for another. Now if we consider human nature as it is, and the utmost development of it that on positive grounds is possible, the conditions that can produce the requisite self-sacrifice will be found to be altogether wanting. The future we are to labour for, even when viewed in its brightest light, will only excel the present in having fewer miseries. So far as its happiness goes it will be distinctly less intense. It will, as we have seen already, be but a vapid consummation at its best; and the more vividly it is brought before us in imagination, the less likely shall we be to 'struggle, groan, and agonize,' for the sake of hastening it in reality. It will do nothing, at any rate, to increase the tendency to self-sacrifice that is now at work in the world; and this, though startling us now and then by some spasmodic manifestation, is not strong enough to have much general effect on the present; still less will it have more effect on the future. Vicarious happiness as a rule is only possible when the object gained for another is enormously greater than the object lost by self; and it is not always possible even then: whilst when the gains on either side are nearly equal, it ceases altogether. And necessarily so. If it did not, everything would be at a dead-lock. Life would be a perpetual holding back, instead of a pushing forward. Everyone would be waiting at the door, and saying to everyone else, 'After you.' But all these practical considerations are entirely forgotten by the positivists. They live in a world of their own imagining, in which all the rules of this world are turned upside down. There, the defeated candidate in an election would be radiant at his rival's victory. When a will was read, the anxiety of each relative would be that he or she should be excluded in favour of the others; or more probably still that they should be all excluded in favour of a hospital. Two rivals, in love with the same woman, would be each anxious that his own suit might be thwarted. And a man would gladly involve himself in any ludicrous misfortune, because he knew that the sight of his catastrophe would rejoice his whole circle of friends. The course of human progress, in fact, would be one gigantic donkey-race, in which those were the winners who were farthest off from the prize.

We have but to state the matter in terms of common life, to see how impossible is the only condition of things that would make the positive system practicable. The first wonder that suggests itself, is how so grotesque a conception could ever have originated. But its genesis is not far to seek. The positivists do not postulate any new elements in human nature, but the reduction of some, elimination of others, and the magnifying of others. And they actually find cases where this process has been effected. But they quite forget the circumstances that have made such an event possible. They forget that in their very nature they have been altogether exceptional and transitory; and that it is impossible to construct a Utopia in which they shall exist at all. We can, for instance, no doubt point to Leonidas and the three hundred as specimens of what human heroism can rise to; and we can point to the Stoics as specimens of human self-control. But to make a new Thermopylæ we want a new Barbarian; and before we can recoil from temptation as the Stoics did, we must make pleasure as perilous and as terrible as it was under the Roman emperors. Such developments of humanity are at their very essence abnormal; and to suppose that they could ever become the common type of character, would be as absurd as to suppose that all mankind could be kings. I will take another instance that is more to the point yet. A favourite positivist parable is that of the miser. The miser in the first place desires gold because it can buy pleasure. Next he comes to desire it more than the pleasure it can buy. In the same way, it is said, men can be taught to desire virtue by investing it with the attractions of the end, to which, strictly speaking it is no more than the means. But this parable really disproves the very possibility it is designed to illustrate. It is designed to illustrate the possibility of our choosing actions that will give pleasure to others, in contradistinction to actions that will give pleasure to ourselves. But the miser desires gold for an exactly opposite reason. He desires it as potential selfishness, not as potential philanthropy. Secondly, we are to choose the actions in question because they will make us happy. But the very name we give the miser shows that the analogous choice in his case makes him miserable. Thirdly, the material miser is an exceptional character; there is no known means by which it can be made more common; and with the moral miser the case will be just the same. Lastly, if such a character be barely producible even in the present state of the world, much less will it be producible when human capacities shall have been curtailed by positivism, when the pleasures that the gold of virtue represents are less intense than at present, and the value of the coveted coin is indefinitely depreciated.

Much more might be added to the same purpose, but enough has been said already to make these two points clear:—firstly, that the positive system, if it is to do any practical work in the world, requires that the whole human character shall be profoundly altered; and secondly, that the required alteration is one that may indeed be dreamt about, but which can never possibly be made. Even were it made, the results would not be splendid; but no matter how splendid they might be, this is of no possible moment to us. There are few things on which it is idler to speculate than the issues of impossible contingencies. And the positivists would be talking just as much to the purpose as they do now, were they to tell us how fast we should travel supposing we had wings, or what deep water we could wade through if we were twenty-four feet high. These last, indeed, are just the suppositions that they do make. Between our human nature and the nature they desiderate there is a deep and fordless river, over which they can throw no bridge, and all their talk supposes that we shall be able to fly or wade across it, or else that it will dry up of itself.

Rusticus expectat dum defluat amnis, at ille
Labitur et labetur, in omne volubilis ævum.
So utterly grotesque and chimerical is this whole positive theory of progress, that, as an outcome of the present age, it seems little short of a miracle. Professing to embody what that age considers its special characteristics, what it really embodies is the most emphatic negation of these. It professes to rest on experience, and yet no Christian legend ever contradicted experience more. It professes to be sustained by proof, and yet the professions of no conjuring quack ever appealed more exclusively to credulity.

Its appearance, however, will cease to be wonderful, and its real significance will become more apparent, if we consider the class of thinkers who have elaborated and popularised it. They have been men and women, for the most part, who have had the following characteristics in common. Their early training has been religious;[28] their temperaments have been naturally grave and earnest; they have had few strong passions; they have been brought up knowing little of what is commonly called the world; their intellects have been vigorous and active; and finally they have rejected in maturity the religion by which all their thoughts have been coloured. The result has been this. The death of their religion has left a quantity of moral emotions without an object; and this disorder of the moral emotions has left their mental energies without a leader. A new object instantly becomes a necessity. They are ethical Don Quixotes in want of a Dulcinea; the best they can find is happiness and the progress of Humanity; and to this their imagination soon gives the requisite glow. Their strong intellects, their activity, and their literary culture each supplements the power that it undoubtedly does give, with a sense of knowing the world that is altogether fictitious. They imagine that their own narrow lives, their own feeble temptations, and their own exceptional ambitions represent the universal elements of human life and character; and they thus expect that an object which has really been but the creature of an impulse in themselves, will be the creator of a like impulse in others; and that in the case of others, it will revolutionise the whole natural character, whereas it has only been a symbol of it in their own.

Most of our positive moralists, at least in this country, have been and are people of such excellent character, and such earnest and high purpose, that there is something painful in having to taunt them with an ignorance which is not their own fault, and which must make their whole position ridiculous. The charge, however, is one that it is quite necessary to make, as we shall never properly estimate their system if we pass it over. It will be said, probably, that the simplicity as to worldly matters I attribute to them, so far from telling against them, is really essential to their character as moral teachers. And to moral teachers of a certain kind it may be essential. But it is not so to them. The religious moralist might well instruct the world, though he knew little of its ways and passions; for the aim of his teaching was to withdraw men from the world. But the aim of the positive moralist is precisely opposite; it is to keep men in the world. It is not to teach men to despise this life, but to adore it. The positions of the two moralists are in fact the exact converses of each other. For the divine, earth is an illusion, heaven a reality; for the positivist, earth is a reality, and heaven an illusion. The former in his retirement studied intensely the world that he thought real, and he could do this the better for being not distracted by the other. The positivists imitate the divine in neglecting what they think is an illusion; but they do not attempt to imitate him in studying what they think is the reality. The consequence is, as I have just been pointing out, that the world they live in and to which alone their system could be applicable, is a world of their own creation, and its bloodless populations are all of them idola specûs.

If we will but think all this calmly over, and try really to sympathise with the position of these poor enthusiasts, we shall soon see their system in its true light, and shall learn at once to realise and to excuse its fatuity. We shall see that it either has no meaning whatever, or that its meaning is one that its authors have already repudiated, and only do not recognise now, because they have so inadequately re-expressed it. We shall see that their system has no motive power at all in it, or that its motive power is simply the theistic faith they rejected, now tied up in a sack and left to flounder instead of walking upright. We shall see that their system is either nothing, or that it is a mutilated reproduction of the very thing it professes to be superseding. Once set it upon its own professed foundations, and the entire quasi-religious structure, with its visionary hopes, its impossible enthusiasms—all its elaborate apparatus for enlarging the single life, and the generation that surrounds it, falls to earth instantly like a castle of cards. We are left simply each of us with our own lives, and with the life about us, amplified indeed to a certain extent by sympathy, but to a certain extent only—an extent whose limits we are quite familiar with from experience, and which positivism, if it tends to move them at all, can only narrow, and can by no possibility extend. We are left with this life, changed only in one way. It will have nothing added to it, but it will have much taken from it. Everything will have gone that is at present keenest in it—joys and miseries as well. In this way positivism is indeed an engine of change, and may inaugurate if not complete a most momentous kind of progress. That progress is the gradual de-religionizing of life, the slow sublimating out of it of its concrete theism—the slow destruction of its whole moral civilisation. And as this progress continues there will not only fade out of the human consciousness the things I have before dwelt on—all capacity for the keener pains and pleasures, but there will fade out of it also that strange sense which is the union of all these—the white light woven of all these rays; that is, the vague but deep sense of some special dignity in ourselves—a sense which we feel to be our birthright, inalienable except by our own act and deed; a sense which, at present, in success sobers us, and in failure sustains us, and which is visible more or less distinctly in our manners, in our bearing, and even in the very expression of the human countenance: it is, in other words, the sense that life is worth living, not accidentally but essentially. And as this sense goes its place will be taken by one precisely opposite—the sense that life, in so far as it is worth living at all, is worth living not essentially, but accidentally; that it depends entirely upon what of its pleasures we can each one of us realise; that it will vary as a positive quantity, like wealth, and that it may become also a various quantity, like poverty; and that behind and beyond these vicissitudes it can have no abiding value.

To realise fully a state of things like this is for us not possible. But we can, however, understand something of its nature. I conceive those to be altogether wrong who say that such a state would be one of any wild license, or anything that we should call very revolting depravity. Offences, certainly, that we consider the most abominable would doubtless be committed continually and as matters of course. Such a feeling as shame about them would be altogether unknown. But the normal forms of passion would remain, I conceive, the most important; and it is probable, that though no form of vice would have the least anathema attached to it, the rage for the sexual pleasures would be far less fierce than it is in many cases now. The sort of condition to which the world would be tending would be a condition rather of dulness than what we, in our parlance, should now call degradation. Indeed the state of things to which the positive view of life seems to promise us, and which to some extent it is actually now bringing on us, is exactly what was predicted long ago, with an accuracy that seems little less than inspired, at the end of Pope's Dunciad.

In vain, in vain: the all-composing hour
Resistless falls! the muse obeys the power.
She comes! she comes! the sable throne behold
Of night primæval and of chaos old.

Before her, fancy's gilded clouds decay,
And all its varying rainbows die away.
Wit shoots in vain its momentary fires,
The meteor drops, and in a flash expires.
As one by one, at dread Medea's strain,
The sickening stars fade off the ethereal plain;
As Argus' eyes, by Hermes' wand oppress'd
Clos'd one by one to everlasting rest;
Thus, at her felt approach and secret might,
Art after art goes out, and all is night.
See skulking truth to her old cavern fled,
Mountains of casuistry heap'd o'er her head.
Philosophy, that lean'd on heaven before,
Shrinks to her second cause, and is no more.
Physic of metaphysic begs defence,
And metaphysic calls for aid on sense!
See mystery to mathematics fly.
In vain: they gaze, turn giddy, rave, and die.
Religion, blushing, veils her sacred fires;
And, unawares, morality expires.
Nor public flame, nor private, dares to shine,
Nor human spark is left, nor glimpse divine.
Lo! thy dread empire, Chaos! is restor'd,
Light dies before thy uncreating word,
Thy hand, great Anarch! lets the curtain fall;
And universal darkness buries all.

Dr. Johnson said that these verses were the noblest in English poetry. Could he have read them in our day, and have realised with what a pitiful accuracy their prophecy might soon begin to fulfil itself, he would probably have been too busy with dissatisfaction at the matter of it to have any time to spare for an artistic approbation of the manner.

[27] Mr. Frederic Harrison.

[28] The case of J. S. Mill may seem at first sight to be an exception to this. But it is really not so. Though he was brought up without any religious teaching, yet the severe and earnest influences of his childhood would have been impossible except in a religious country. He was in fact brought up in an atmosphere (if I may borrow with a slight change a phrase of Professor Huxley's) of Puritanism minus Christianity. It may be remembered farther that Mill says of himself, 'I am one of the very few examples of one who has not thrown off religious belief, but never had it.'

Is Life Worth Living? By William Hurrell Mallock

CHAPTER VIII.

THE PRACTICAL PROSPECT.

Not from the stars do I my judgment pluck....
Nor can I fortune to brief minutes tell.
Shakespeare, Sonnet XIV.

The prospects I have been just describing as the goal of positive progress will seem, no doubt, to many to be quite impossible in its cheerlessness. If the future glory of our race was a dream, not worth dwelling on, much more so, they will say, is such a future abasement of it as this. They will say that optimism may at times have perhaps been over-sanguine, but that this was simply the exuberance of health; whereas pessimism is, in its very nature, the gloom and languor of a disease.

Now with much of this view of the matter I entirely agree. I admit that the prospect I have described may be an impossible one; personally, I believe it is so. I admit also that pessimism is the consciousness of disease, confessing itself. But the significance of these admissions is the very opposite of what it is commonly supposed to be. They do not make the pessimism I have been arguing one whit less worthy of attention; on the contrary, they make it more worthy. This is the point on which I may most readily be misunderstood. I will therefore try to make my meaning as clear as possible.

Pessimism, then, represents, to the popular mind, a philosophy or view of life the very name of which is enough to condemn it. The popular mind, however, overlooks one important point. Pessimism is a vague word. It does not represent one philosophy, but several; and before we, in any case, reject its claims on our attention, we should take care to see what its exact meaning is.

The views of life it includes may be classified in two ways. In the first place, they are either what we may call critical pessimisms or prospective pessimisms: of which the thesis of the first is that human life is essentially evil; and of the second, that whatever human life may be now, its tendency is to get worse instead of better. The one is the denial of human happiness; the other the denial of human hope. But there is a second classification to make, traversing this one, and far more important. Pessimism may be either absolute or hypothetical. The first of these maintains its theses as statements of actual facts; the second, which is, of its nature, prospective mainly, only maintains them as statements of what will be facts, in the event of certain possible though it may be remote contingencies.

Now, absolute pessimism, whether it be critical or prospective, can be nothing, in the present state of the world, but an exhibition of ill temper or folly. It is hard to imagine a greater waste of ingenuity than the attempts that have been made sometimes to deduce from the nature of pain and pleasure, that the balance in life must be always in favour of the former, and that life itself is necessarily and universally an evil. Let the arguments be never so elaborate, they are blown away like cobwebs by a breath of open-air experience. Equally useless are the attempts to predict the gloom of the future. Such predictions either mean nothing, or else they are mere loose conjectures, suggested by low spirits or disappointment. They are of no philosophic or scientific value; and though in some cases they may give literary expression to moods already existing, they will never produce conviction in minds that would else be unconvinced. The gift of prophecy as to general human history is not a gift that any philosophy can bestow. It could only be acquired through a superhuman inspiration which is denied to man or through a superhuman sagacity which is never attained by him.

The hypothetical pessimism that is contained in my arguments is a very different thing from this, and far humbler. It makes no foolish attempts to say anything general about the present, or anything absolute about the future. As to the future, it only takes the absolute things that have been said by others; and not professing any certainty about their truth, merely explains their meaning. It deals with a certain change in human beliefs, now confidently predicted; but it does not say that this prediction will be fulfilled. It says only that if it be, a change, not at present counted on, will be effected in human life. It says that human life will degenerate if the creed of positivism be ever generally accepted; but it not only does not say that it ever will be accepted by everybody: rather, it emphatically points out that as yet it has been accepted fully by nobody. The positive school say that their view of life is the only sound one. They boast that it is founded on the rock of fact, not on the sand-bank of sentiment; that it is the final philosophy, that will last as long as man lasts, and that very soon it will have seen the extinction of all the others. It is the positivists who are the prophets, not I. My aim has been not to confirm the prophecy, but to explain its meaning; and my arguments will be all the more opportune at the present moment, the more reason we have to think the prophecy false.

It may be asked why, if we think it false, we should trouble our heads about it. And the answer to this is to be found in the present age itself. Whatever may be the future fate of positive thought, whatever confidence may be felt by any of us that it cannot in the long run gain a final hold upon the world, its present power and the present results of it cannot be overlooked. That degradation of life that I have been describing as the result of positivism—of what the age we live in calls the only rational view of things—may indeed never be completed; but let us look carefully around us, and we shall see that it is already begun. The process, it is true, is at present not very apparent; or if it is, its nature is altogether mistaken. This, however, only makes it more momentous; and the great reason why it is desirable to deal so rudely with the optimist system of the positivists is that it lies like a misty veil over the real surface of facts, and conceals the very change that it professes to make impossible. It is a kind of moral chloroform, which, instead of curing an illness, only makes us fatally unconscious of its most alarming symptoms.

But though an effort be thus required to realise our true condition, it is an effort which, before all things, we ought to make; and which, if we try, we can all make readily. A little careful memory, a little careful observation, will open the eyes of most of us to the real truth of things; it will reveal to us a spectacle that is indeed appalling, and the more candidly we survey it, the more shall we feel aghast at it. To begin, then, let us once more consider two notorious facts: first, that over all the world at the present day a denial is spreading itself of all religions dogmas, more complete than has ever before been known; and, secondly, that in spite of this speculative denial, and in the places where it has done its work most thoroughly, a mass of moral earnestness seems to survive untouched. I do not attempt to deny the fact; I desire, on the contrary, to draw all attention to it. But the condition in which it survives is commonly not in the least realised. The class of men concerned with it are like soldiers who may be fighting more bravely perhaps than ever; but who are fighting, though none observe it, with the death-wound under their uniforms. Of all the signs of the times, these high-minded unbelievers are thought to be the most reassuring; but really they are the very reverse of this. The reason why their true condition has passed unnoticed is, that it is a condition that is naturally silent, and that has great difficulty in finding a mouthpiece. The only two parties who have had any interest in commenting on it have been the very parties least able to understand, and most certain to distort it. They have been either the professed champions of theism, or else the visionary optimists of positivism; the former of whom have had no sympathy with positive principles, and the latter no discernment of their results. The class of men we are considering are equally at variance with both of these; they agree with each in one respect, and in another they agree with neither. They agree with the one that religious belief is false; they agree with the other that unbelief is miserable. What wonder then that they should have kept their condition to themselves? Nearly all public dealing with it has been left to men who can praise the only doctrines that they can preach as true, or who else can condemn as false the doctrines that they deplore as mischievous. As for the others, whose mental and moral convictions are at variance, they have neither any heart to proclaim the one, nor any intellectual standpoint from which to proclaim the other. Their only impulse is to struggle and to endure in silence. Let us, however, try to intrude upon their privacy, even though it be rudely and painfully, and see what their real state is; for it is these men who are the true product of the present age, its most special and distinguishing feature, and the first-fruits of what we are told is to be the philosophy of the enlightened future.

To begin, then, let us remember what these men were when Christians; and we shall be better able to realise what they are now. They were men who believed firmly in the supreme and solemn importance of life, in the privilege that it was to live, despite all temporal sorrow. They had a rule of conduct which would guide them, they believed, to the true end of their being—to an existence satisfying and excellent beyond anything that imagination could suggest to them; they had the dread of a corresponding ruin to fortify themselves in their struggle against the wrong; and they had a God ever present, to help and hear, and take pity on them. And yet even thus, selfishness would beset the most unselfish, and weariness the most determined. How hard the battle was, is known to all; it has been the most prominent commonplace in human thought and language. The constancy and the strength of temptation, and the insidiousness of the arguments it was supported by, has been proverbial. To explain away the difference between good and evil, to subtly steal its meaning out of long-suffering and self-denial, and, above all, to argue that in sinning 'we shall not surely die,' a work which was supposed to belong especially to the devil, has been supposed to have been accomplished by him with a success continually irresistible. What, then, is likely to be the case now, with men who are still beset with the same temptations, when not only they have no hell to frighten, no heaven to allure, and no God to help them; but when all the arguments that they once felt belonged to the father of lies, are pressed on them from every side as the most solemn and universal truths? Thus far the result has been a singular one. With an astonishing vigour the moral impetus still survives the cessation of the forces that originated and sustained it; and in many cases there is no diminution of it traceable, so far as action goes. This, however, is only true, for the most part, of men advanced in years, in whom habits of virtue have grown strong, and whose age, position, and circumstances secure them from strong temptation. To see the real work of positive thought we must go to younger men, whose characters are less formed, whose careers are still before them, and on whom temptation of all kinds has stronger hold. We shall find such men with the sense of virtue equally vivid in them, and the desire to practise it probably far more passionate; but the effect of positive thought on them we shall see to be very different.

Now, the positive school itself will say that such men have all they need. They confessedly have conscience left to them—the supernatural moral judgment, that is, as applied to themselves—which has been analysed, but not destroyed; and the position of which, we are told, has been changed only by its being set on a foundation of fact, instead of a foundation of superstition. Mill said that having learnt what the sunset clouds were made of, he still found that he admired them as much as ever; 'therefore,' he said, 'I saw at once that there was nothing to be feared from analysis.' And this is exactly what the positive school say of conscience. A shallower falsehood, however, it is not easy to conceive. It is true that conscience in one way may, for a time at least, survive any kind of analysis. It may continue, with undiminished distinctness, its old approvals and menaces. But that alone is nothing at all to the point. Conscience is of practical value, not only because it says certain things, but because it says them, as we think, with authority. If its authority goes, and its advice continues, it may indeed molest, but it will no longer direct us. Now, though the voice of conscience may, as the positive school say, survive their analysis of it, its authority will not. That authority has always taken the form of a menace, as well as of an approval; and the menace at any rate, upon all positive principles, is nothing but big words that can break no bones. As soon as we realise it to be but this, its effect must cease instantly. The power of conscience resides not in what we hear it to be, but in what we believe it to be. A housemaid may be deterred from going to meet her lover in the garden, because a howling ghost is believed to haunt the laurels; but she will go to him fast enough when she discovers that the sounds that alarmed her were not a soul in torture, but the cat in love. The case of conscience is exactly analogous to this.

And now let us turn again to the case in question. Men of such a character as I have been just describing may find conscience quite equal to giving a glow, by its approval, to their virtuous wishes; but they will find it quite unequal to sustaining them against their vicious ones; and the more vigorous the intellect of the man, the more feeble will be the power of conscience. When a man is very strongly tempted to do a thing which he believes to be wrong, it is almost inevitable that he will test to the utmost the reasons of this belief; or if he does not do this before he yields to the temptation, yet if he does happen to yield to it, he will certainly do so after. Thus, unless we suppose human nature to be completely changed, and all our powers of observation completely misleading, the inward condition of the class in question is this. However calm the outer surface of their lives may seem, under the surface there is a continual discord; and also, though they alone may perceive it, a continued decadence. In various degrees they all yield to temptation; all men in the vigour of their manhood do; and conscience still fills them with its old monitions and reproaches. But it cannot enforce obedience. They feel it to be the truth, but at the same time they know it to be a lie; and though they long to be coerced by it, they find it cannot coerce them. Reason, which was once its minister, is now the tribune of their passions, and forbids them, in times of passion, to submit to it. They are not suffered to forget that it is not what it says it is, that

It never came from on high,
And never rose from below:
and they cannot help chiding themselves with the irrepressible self-reproach,

Am I to be overawed

By what I cannot but know,
Is a juggle born of the brain?

Thus their conscience, though not stifled, is dethroned; it is become a fugitive Pretender; and that part of them that would desire its restoration is set down as an intellectual malignant, powerless indeed to restore its sovereign.

Invalidasque tibi tendens, heu non tua, palmas.

Conscience, in short, as soon as its power is needed, is like their own selves dethroned within themselves, wringing its hands over a rebellion it is powerless to suppress. And then, when the storm is over, when the passions again subside, and their lives once more return to their wonted channels, it can only come back humbly and dejected, and give them in a timid voice a faint, dishonoured blessing.

Such lives as these are all of them really in a state of moral consumption. The disease in its earlier stage is a very subtle one; and it may not be generally fatal for years, or even for generations. But it is a disease that can be transmitted from parent to child; and its progress is none the less sure because it is slow; nor is it less fatal and painful because it may often give a new beauty to the complexion. On various constitutions it takes hold in various ways, and its presence is first detected by the sufferer under various trials, and betrayed to the observer by various symptoms. What I have just been describing is the action that is at the root of it; but with the individual it does not always take that form. Often indeed it does; but oftener still perhaps it is discovered not in the helpless yet reluctant yielding to vice, but in the sadness and the despondency with which virtue is practised—in the dull leaden hours of blank endurance or of difficult endeavour; or in the little satisfaction that, when the struggle has ceased, the reward of struggle brings with it.

An earlier, and perhaps more general symptom still, is one that is not personal. It consists not in the way in which men regard themselves, but in the way in which they regard others. In their own case, their habitual desire of right, and their habitual aversion to wrong, may have been enough to keep them from any open breach with conscience, or from putting it to an open shame. But its precarious position is revealed to them when they turn to others. Sin from which they recoil themselves they see committed in the life around them, and they find that it cannot excite the horror or disapproval, which from its supposed nature it should. They find themselves powerless to pass any general judgment, or to extend the law they live by to any beyond themselves. The whole prospect that environs them has become morally colourless; and they discern in their attitude towards the world without, what it must one day come to be towards the world within. A state of mind like this is no dream. It is a malady of the modern world—a malady of our own generation, which can escape no eyes that will look for it. It is betraying itself every moment around us, in conversation, in literature, and in legislation.

Such, then, is the condition of that large and increasing class on which modern thought is beginning to do its work. Its work must be looked for here, and not in narrower quarters; not amongst professors and lecturers, but amongst the busy crowd about us; not on the platforms of institutions, or in the lay sermons of specialists, but amongst politicians, artists, sportsmen, men of business, lovers—in 'the tides of life, and in the storm of action'—amongst men who have their own way to force or choose in the world, and their daily balance to strike between self-denial and pleasure—on whom the positive principles have been forced as true, and who have no time or talent to do anything else but live by them. It is amongst these that we must look to see what such principles really result in; and of these we must choose not those who would welcome license, but those who long passionately to live by law. It is the condition of such men that I have been just describing. Its characteristics are vain self-reproach, joyless commendation, weary struggle, listless success, general indifference, and the prospect that if matters are going thus badly with them, they will go even worse with their children.

Such a spectacle certainly is not one that has much promise for the optimist; and the more we consider it, the more sad and ominous will it appear to us. Indeed, when the present age shall realise its own condition truly, the dejection of which it is slowly growing conscious may perhaps give way to despair. This condition, however, is so portentous that it is difficult to persuade ourselves that it is what it seems to be, and that it is not a dream. But the more steadily we look at it, the more real will its appalling features appear to us. We are literally in an age to which history can show no parallel, and which is new to the experience of humanity; and though the moral dejection we have been dwelling on may have had many seeming counterparts in other times, this is, as it were, solid substance, whereas they were only shadows. I have pointed out already in my first chapter how unexampled is the state in which the world now finds itself; but we will dwell once again upon its more general features. Within less than a century, distance has been all but annihilated, and the earth has practically, and to the imagination, been reduced to a fraction of its former size. Its possible resources have become mean and narrow, set before us as matters of every-day statistics. All the old haze of wonder is melting away from it; and the old local enthusiasms, which depended so largely on ignorance and isolation, are melting likewise. Knowledge has accumulated in a way never before dreamed of. The fountains of the past seem to have been broken up, and to be pouring all their secrets into the consciousness of the present. For the first time man's wide and varied history has become a coherent whole to him. Partly a cause and partly a result of this, a new sense has sprung up in him—an intense self-consciousness as to his own position; and his entire view of himself is undergoing a vague change: whilst the positive basis on which knowledge has been placed, has given it a constant and coercive force, and has made the same change common to the whole civilised world. Thought and feeling amongst the western nations are conforming to a single pattern: they are losing their old chivalrous character, their possibilities of isolated conquest and intellectual adventure. They are settling down into a uniform mass, that moves or stagnates like a modern army, and whose alternative lines of march have been mapped out beforehand. Such is the condition of the western world; and the western world is beginning now, at all points, to bear upon the east. Thus opinions that the present age is forming for itself have a weight and a volume that opinions never before possessed. They are the first beginnings, not of natural, or of social, but of human opinion—an œcumenical self-consciousness on the part of man as to his own prospects and his own position. The great question is, what shape finally will this dawning self-consciousness take? Will it contain in it that negation of the supernatural which our positive assertions are at present supposed to necessitate? If so, then it is not possible to conceive that this last development of humanity, this stupendous break from the past which is being accomplished by our understanding of it, will not be the sort of break which takes place when a man awakes from a dream, and finds all that he most prized vanished from him. It is impossible to conceive that this awakening, this discovery by man of himself, will not be the beginning of his decadence; that it will not be the discovery on his part that he is a lesser and a lower thing than he thought he was, and that his condition will not sink till it tallies with his own opinion of it.

If this be really the case, we shall not be able to dispose of pessimism by calling it a disease; for the disease will be real and universal, and pessimism will be nothing but the scientific description of it. The pessimist is only silenced by being called diseased, when it is meant that the disease imputed to him is either hypochondriacal or peculiar to himself. But in the present case the disease is real, deep-seated, and extending steadily. The only question for us is, is it curable or incurable? This the event alone can answer: but as no future can be produced but through the agency of the present, the event, to a certain extent, must be in our own hands. For us, at any rate, the first thing to be done is to face boldly our own present condition, and the causes that are producing it. To become alive to our danger is the one way to escape from it. But the danger is at present felt rather than known. The class of men we are considering are conscious, as Mr. Matthew Arnold says, 'of a void that mines the breast;' but each thinks that this is a fancy only, and hardly dares communicate it to his fellows. Here and there, however, by accident, it is already finding unintended expression; and signs come to the surface of the vague distrust and misgiving that are working under it. The form it takes amongst the general masses that are affected by it is, as might be expected, practical rather than analytical. They are conscious of the loss that the loss of faith is to them; and more or less coherently they long for its recovery. Outwardly, indeed, they may often sneer at it; but outward signs in such matters are very deceiving. Much of the bitter and arrogant certitude to be found about us in the expression of unbelief, is really like the bitterness of a woman against her lover, which has not been the cause of her resolving to leave him, but which has been caused by his having left her. In estimating what is really the state of feeling about us, we must not look only at the surface. We must remember that deep feeling often expresses itself by contradicting itself; also that it often exists where it is not expressed at all, or where it betrays rather than expresses itself; and, further, that during the hours of common intercourse, it tends, for the time being, to disappear. People cannot be always exclaiming in drawing-rooms that they have lost their Lord; and the fact may be temporarily forgotten because they have lost their portmanteau. All serious reflections are like reflections in water—a pebble will disturb them, and make a dull pond sparkle. But the sparkle dies, and the reflection comes again. And there are many about us, though they never confess their pain, and perhaps themselves hardly like to acknowledge it, whose hearts are aching for the religion that they can no longer believe in. Their lonely hours, between the intervals of gaiety, are passed with barren and sombre thoughts; and a cry rises to their lips but never passes them.

Amongst such a class it is somehow startling to find the most unlikely people at times placing themselves. Professor Clifford, for instance, who of all our present positivists is most uproarious in his optimism, has yet admitted that the religion he invites us to trample on is, under certain forms, an ennobling and sustaining thing; and for such theism as that of Charles Kingsley's he has expressed his deepest reverence. Again, there is Professor Huxley. He denies with the most dogmatic and unbending severity any right to man to any supernatural faith; and he 'will not for a moment admit' that our higher life will suffer in consequence.[29] And yet 'the lover of moral beauty,' he says wistfully, 'struggling through a world of sorrow and sin, is surely as much the stronger for believing that sooner or later a vision of perfect peace and goodness will burst upon him, as the toiler up a mountain for the belief that beyond crag and snow lie home and rest.' And he adds, as we have seen already, that could a faith like what he here indicates be placed upon a firm basis, mankind would cling to it as 'tenaciously as ever a drowning sailor did to a hen-coop.' But all this wide-spread and increasing feeling is felt at present to be of no avail. The wish to believe is there; but the belief is as far off as ever. There is a power in the air around us by which man's faith seems paralysed. The intellect, we were thinking but now, had acquired a new vigour and a clearer vision; but the result of this growth is, with many, to have made it an incubus, and it lies upon all their deepest hopes and wishes

Like a weight
Heavy as frost, and deep almost as life.
Such is the condition of mind that is now spreading rapidly, and which, sooner or later, we must look steadily in the face. Nor is it confined to those who are its direct victims. Those who still cling, and cling firmly, to belief are in an indirect way touched by it. Religion cannot fail to be changed by the neighbourhood of irreligion. If it is persecuted,

it may burn up with greater fervour; but if it is not persecuted, it must in some measure be chilled. Believers and unbelievers, separated as they are by their tenets, are yet in these days mixed together in all the acts and relations of life. They are united by habits, by blood, and by friendship, and they are each obliged continually to ignore or excuse what they hold to be the errors of the other. In a state of things like this, it is plain that the conviction of believers can have neither the fierce intensity that belongs to a minority under persecution, nor the placid confidence that belongs to an overwhelming majority. They can neither hate the unbelievers, for they daily live in amity with them, nor despise altogether their judgment, for the most eminent thinkers of the day belong to them. By such conditions as these the strongest faith cannot fail to be affected. As regards the individuals who retain it, it may not lose its firmness, but it must lose something of its fervour; and as regards its own future hold upon the human race, it is faith no longer, but is anxious doubt, or, at best, a desperate trust. Dr. Newman has pointed out how even the Pope has recognised in the sedate and ominous rise of our modern earth-born positivism some phenomenon vaster and of a different nature from the outburst of a petulant heresy; he seems to recognise it as a belligerent rather than a rebel.30 'One thing,' says Dr. Newman, 'except by an almost miraculous interposition, cannot be; and that is a return to the universal religious sentiment, the public opinion, of the mediæval time. The Pope himself calls those centuries "the ages of faith." Such endemic faith may certainly be decreed for some future time; but as far as we have the means of judging at present, centuries must run out first.'31

In this last sentence is indicated the vast and universal question, which the mind of humanity is gathering itself together to ask—will the faith that we are so fast losing ever again revive for us? And my one aim in this book has been to demonstrate that the entire future tone of life, and the entire course of future civilisation, depends on the answer which this question receives.

There is, however, this further point to consider. Need the answer we are speaking of be definite and universal? or can we look forward to its remaining undecided till the end of time? Now I have already tried to make it evident that for the individual, at any rate, it must by-and-by be definite one way or the other. The thorough positive thinker will not be able to retain in supreme power principles which have no positive basis. He cannot go on adoring a hunger which he knows can never be satisfied, or cringing before fears which he knows will never be realised. And even if this should for a time be possible, his case will be worse, not better. Conscience, if it still remains with him, will remain not as a living thing—a severe but kindly guide—but as the menacing ghost of the religion he has murdered, and which comes to embitter degradation, not to raise it. The moral life, it is true, will still exist for him, but it will probably, in literal truth,

Creep on a broken wing

Through cells of madness, haunts of horror and fear.

But a state of things like this can hardly be looked forward to as conceivably of any long continuance. Religion would come back, or conscience would go. Nor do I think that the future which Dr. Newman seems to anticipate can be regarded as probable either. He seems to anticipate a continuance side by side of faith and positivism, each with their own adherents, and fighting a ceaseless battle in which neither gains the victory. I venture to submit that the new forms now at work in the world are not forms that will do their work by halves. When once the age shall have mastered them, they will be either one thing or the other—they will be either impotent or omnipotent. Their public exponents at present boast that they will be omnipotent; and more and more the world about us is beginning to believe the boast. But the world feels uneasily that the import of it will be very different from what we are assured it is. One English writer, indeed, on the positive side, has already seen clearly what the movement really means, whose continuance and whose consummation he declares to us to be a necessity. 'Never,' he says, 'in the history of man has so terrific a calamity befallen the race as that which all who look may now behold, advancing as a deluge, black with destruction, resistless in might, uprooting our most cherished hopes, engulfing our most precious creed, and burying our highest life in mindless desolation.'[32]

The question I shall now proceed to is the exact causes of this movement, and the chances and the powers that the human race has of resisting it.

Is Life Worth Living? By William Hurrell Mallock

CHAPTER IX.

THE LOGIC OF SCIENTIFIC NEGATION.

I am Sir Oracle,
And when I ope my mouth let no dog bark.
Before beginning to analyse the forces that are decomposing religious belief, it will be well to remark briefly on the means by which these forces are applied to the world at large. To a certain extent they are applied directly; that is, many of the facts that are now becoming obvious the common sense of all men assimilates spontaneously, and derives, unbidden, its own doubts or denials from them. But the chief power of positivism is derived otherwise. It is derived not directly from the premises that it puts before us, but from the intellectual prestige of its exponents, who, to the destruction of private judgment, are forcing on us their own personal conclusions from them. This prestige, indeed, is by no means to be wondered at. If men ever believed a teacher 'for his works' sake,' the positive school is associated with enough signs and wonders. All those astonishing powers that man has acquired in this century are with much justice claimed by it as its works and gifts. The whole sensuous surroundings of our lives are its subjects, and are doing it daily homage; and there is not a conquest over distance, disease, or darkness that does not seem to bear witness to its intellectual supremacy. The opinion, therefore, that is now abroad in the world is that the positive school are the monopolists of unbiassed reason; that reason, therefore, is altogether fatal to religion; and that those who deny this, only do so through ignorance or through wilful blindness. As long as this opinion lasts, the revival of faith is hopeless. What we are now about to examine is, how far this opinion is well founded.

The arguments which operate against religion with the leaders of modern thought, and through their intellectual example on the world at large, divide themselves into three classes, and are derived from three distinct branches of thought and study. They may be distinguished as physical, moral, and historical. Few of these arguments, taken separately, can be called altogether new. Their new power has been caused by the simultaneous filling up and completion of all of them; by their transmutation from filmy visions into massive and vast realities; from unauthorised misgivings into the most rigid and compelling of demonstrations: and still more, by the brilliant and sudden annihilation of the most obvious difficulties, which till very lately had neutralised and held their power in check.

Of these three sets of arguments, the two first bear upon all religion, whilst the third bears upon it only as embodied in some exclusive form. Thus the physicist argues, for example, that consciousness being a function of the brain, unless the universe be a single brain itself, there can be no conscious God.33 The moral philosopher argues that sin and misery being so prevalent, there can be no Almighty and all-merciful God. And the historian argues that all alleged revelations can be shown to have had analogous histories; and that therefore, even if God exists, there is no one religion through which He has specially revealed Himself. These are rough specimens solubly, so far as observation can carry us, mind with matter. The great gulf between the two has at last been spanned. The bridge across it, that was so long seen in dreams and despaired of, has been thrown triumphantly—a solid compact fabric, on which a hundred intellectual masons are still at work, adding stone on ponderous stone to it. Science, to put the matter in other words, has accomplished these three things. Firstly, to use the words of a well-known writer, 'it has established a functional relation to exist between every fact of thinking, willing, or feeling, on the one side, and some molecular change in the body on the other side.' Secondly, it has connected, through countless elusive stages, this organic human body 211with the universal lifeless matter. And thirdly, it claims to have placed the universal matter itself in a new position for us, and to exhibit all forms of life as developed from it, through its own spontaneous motion. Thus for the first time, beyond the reach of question, the entire sensible universe is brought within the scope of the physicist. Everything that is, is matter moving. Life itself is nothing but motion of an infinitely complex kind. It is matter in its finest ferment. The first traceable beginnings of it are to be found in the phenomenon of crystallisation; we have there, we are told by the highest scientific authority, 'the first gropings of the so-called vital force;' and we learn from the same quarter, that between these and the brain of Christ there is a difference in degree only, not in kind: they are each of them 'an assemblage of molecules, acting and re-acting according to law.' 'We believe,' says Dr. Tyndall, 'that every thought and every feeling has its definite mechanical correlative—that it is accompanied by a certain breaking up and re-marshalling of the atoms of the brain.' And though he of course admits that to trace out the processes in detail is infinitely beyond our powers, yet 'the quality of the problem and of our powers,' he says, 'are, we believe, so related, that a mere expansion of the latter would enable them to cope with the former.' Nowhere is there any break in Nature; and 'supposing,' in Dr. Tyndall's words,212 'a planet carved from the sun, set spinning on an axis, and sent revolving round the sun at a distance equal to that of our earth,' science points to the conclusion that as the mass cooled, it would flower out in places into just such another race as ours—creatures of as large discourse, and, like ourselves, looking before and after. The result is obvious. Every existing thing that we can ever know, or hope to know, in the whole inward as well as in the whole outward world—everything from a star to a thought, or from a flower to an affection, is connected with certain material figures, and with certain mechanical forces. All have a certain bulk and a certain place in space, and could conceivably be made the subjects of some physical experiment. Faith, sanctity, doubt, sorrow, and love, could conceivably be all gauged and detected by some scientific instrument—by a camera or by a spectroscope; and their conditions and their intensity be represented by some sort of diagram.

These marvellous achievements, as I have said, have been often before dreamed of. Now they are accomplished. As applied to natural religion, the effect of them is as follows.

Firstly, with regard to God, they have taken away every external proof of His existence, and, still more, every sign of His daily providence. They destroy them completely at a sudden and single blow, and send them falling about us like so many dead flies. God, as connected with the external world, was conceived of in three ways—as a Mover, as a Designer, and as a Superintendent. In the first two capacities He was required by thought; in the last, He was supposed to be revealed by experience. But now in none of these is He required or revealed longer. So far as thought goes, He has become a superfluity; so far as experience goes, He has become a fanciful suggestion.

Secondly, with regard to man, the life and soul are presented to us, not as an entity distinct from the body, and therefore capable of surviving it, but as a function of it, or the sum of its functions, which has demonstrably grown with its growth, which is demonstrably dependent upon even its minutest changes, and which, for any sign or hint to the contrary, will be dissolved with its dissolution.

A God, therefore, that is the master of matter, and a human soul that is independent of it—any second world, in fact, of alien and trans-material forces, is reduced, on physical grounds, to an utterly unsupported hypothesis. Were this all, however, it would logically have on religion no effect at all. It would supply us with nothing but the barren verbal proposition that the immaterial was not material, or that we could find no trace of it by merely studying matter. Its whole force rests on the following suppressed premiss, that nothing exists but what the study of matter conceivably could reveal to us; or that, in other words, the immaterial equals the nonexistent. The case stands thus. The forces of thought and spirit were supposed formerly to be quite distinct from matter, and to be capable of acting without the least connection with it. Now, it is shown that every smallest revelation of these to us, is accomplished by some local atomic movement, which, on a scientific instrument fine enough, would leave a distinct impression; and thus it is argued that no force is revealed through matter that is not inseparable from the forms revealing it. Here we see the meaning of that great modern axiom, that verification is the test of truth; or that we can build on nothing as certain but what we can prove true. The meaning of the word 'proof' by itself may perhaps be somewhat hazy; but the meaning that positive science attaches to it is plain enough. A fact is only proved when the evidence it rests upon leaves us no room for doubt—when it forces on every mind the same invincible conviction; that is, in other words, when, directly or indirectly, its material equivalent can be impressed upon our bodily senses.

This is the fulcrum of the modern intellectual lever. Ask anyone oppressed and embittered by the want of religion the reason why he does not again embrace it, and the answer will still be this—that there is no proof that it is true. Granting, says Professor Huxley, that a religious creed would be beneficial, 'my next step is to ask for a proof of its dogmas.' And with contemptuous passion another well-known writer, Mr. Leslie Stephen, has classified all beliefs, according as we can prove or not prove them, into realities and empty dreams. 'The ignorant and childish,' he says, 'are hopelessly unable to draw the line between dreamland and reality; but the imagery which takes its rise in the imagination as distinguished from the perceptions, bears indelible traces of its origin in comparative unsubstantiality and vagueness of outline.' And 'now,' he exclaims, turning to the generation around him, 'at last your creed is decaying. People have discovered that you know nothing about it; that heaven and hell belong to dreamland; that the impertinent young curate who tells me that I shall be burnt everlastingly for not sharing his superstition, is just as ignorant as I myself, and that I know as much as my dog.'[34]

Such is that syllogism of the physical sciences which is now supposed to be so invincible against all religion, and which has already gone so far towards destroying the world's faith in it. Now as to the minor premiss, that there is no proof of religion, we may concede, at least provisionally, that it is completely true. What it is really important to examine is the major premiss, that we can be certain of nothing that we cannot support by proof. This it is plain does not stand on the same footing as the former, for it is of its very nature not capable of being proved itself. Its foundation is something far less definable—the general character for wisdom of the leading thinkers who have adopted it, and the general acceptance of its consequences by the common sense of mankind.

Now if we examine its value by these tests, the result will be somewhat startling. We find that not only are mankind at large as yet but very partially aware of its consequences, but that its true scope and meaning has not even dawned dimly on the leading thinkers themselves. Few spectacles, indeed, in the whole history of thought are more ludicrous than that of the modern positive school with their great doctrine of verification. They apply it rigorously to one set of facts, and then utterly fail to see that it is equally applicable to another. They apply it to religion, and declare that the dogmas of religion are dreams; but when they pass from the dogmas of religion to those of morality, they not only do not use their test, but unconsciously they denounce it with the utmost vehemence. Thus Mr. Leslie Stephen, in the very essay from which I have just now quoted, not only has recourse, for giving weight to his arguments, to such ethical epithets as low, lofty, and even sacred, but he puts forward as his own motive for speaking, a belief which on his own showing is a dream. That motive, he says, is devotion to truth for its own sake—the only principle that is really worthy of man. His argument is simply this. It is man's holiest and most important duty to discover the truth at all costs, and the one test of truth is physical verification. Here he tells us we find the only high morality, and the men who cling to religious dream-dogmas which they cannot physically verify, can only answer their opponents, says Mr. Stephen, 'by a shriek or a sneer.' 'The sentiment,' he proceeds, 'which the dreamer most thoroughly hates and misunderstands, is the love of truth for its own sake. He cannot conceive why a man should attack a lie simply because it is a lie.' Mr. Stephen is wrong. That is exactly what the dreamer can do, and no one else but he; and Mr. Stephen is himself a dreamer when he writes and feels like this. Why, let me ask him, should the truth be loved? Do the 'perceptions,' which are for him the only valid guides, tell him so? The perceptions tell him, as he expressly says, that the truths of nature, so far as man is concerned with them, are 'harsh' truths. Why should 'harsh' things be loveable? Or supposing Mr. Stephen does love them, why is that love 'lofty'? and why should he so brusquely command all other men to share it? Low and lofty—what has Mr. Stephen to do with words like these? They are part of the language of dreamland, not of real life. Mr. Stephen has no right to them. If he has, he must be able to draw a hard and fast line between them; for if his conceptions of them be 'vague in outline' and 'unsubstantial,' they belong by his own express definition to the land of dreams. But this is what Mr. Stephen, with the solemn imbecility of his school, is quite incapable of seeing. Professor Huxley is in exactly the same case. He says, as we have seen already, that, come what may of it, our highest morality is to follow truth; that the 'lowest depth of immorality' is to pretend to believe what we see no reason for believing;' and that our only proper reasons for belief are some physical, some perceptible evidence. And yet at the same time he says that to 'attempt to upset morality' by the help of the physical sciences is about as rational or as possible as to 'attempt to upset Euclid by the help of the Rig Veda.' Now on Professor Huxley's principles, this last sentence, though it sounds very weighty, is, if so ungracious a word may be allowed me, nothing short of nonsense. It would be the lowest depth of immorality, he says, to believe in God, when we see that there is no physical evidence to justify the belief. And physical science in this way he admits—he indeed proclaims—has upset religion. How then has physical science in the same way failed to upset morality? The foundation of morality, he says, is the belief that truth for its own sake is sacred. But what proof can he discover of this sacredness? Does any positive method of experience or observation so much as tend to suggest it? We have already seen that it does not. What Professor Huxley's philosophy really proves to him is that it is true that nothing is sacred; not that it is a sacred thing to discover the truth.

We saw all this already when we were examining his comparison of the perception of moral beauty to the perception of the heat of ginger. It is the same thing with which we are again dealing now, only we are approaching it from a slightly different point of view.

What we saw before, was that without an assent to the religious dogmas, the moral dogmas can have no logical meaning. We have now seen that even were the two logically independent, they yet belong both of them to the same order of things; and that if our tests of truth prove the former to be illusions, they will, with precisely the same force, prove the same thing of the latter.

But the most crucial test of all we have still to come to, which will put this conclusion in a yet clearer and a more unmistakable light. Thus far what we have seen has amounted to only this—that if science can take from man his religious faith, it leaves him a being without any moral guidance.220 What we shall now see is that, by the same arguments, it will prove him to be not a moral being at all; that it will prove not only that he has no rule by which to direct his will, but also that he has no will to direct.

To understand this we must return to physical science, and to the exact results that have been accomplished by it. We have seen how completely, from one point of view, it has connected mind with matter, and how triumphantly it is supposed to have unified the apparent dualism of things. It has revealed the brain to us as matter in a combination of infinite complexity, which it has reached at last through its own automatic workings; and it has revealed consciousness to us as a function of this brain, and as altogether inseparable from it. But for this, the old dualism now supposed to be obsolete would remain undisturbed. Indeed, if this doctrine were denied, such a dualism would be the only alternative. For every thought, then, that we think, and every feeling or desire that we feel, there takes place in the brain some definite material movement, on the force or figure of which the thoughts and feelings are dependent. Now if physical observations are to be the only things that guide us, one important fact will become at once evident. Matter existed and fermented long before the evolution of mind; mind is not an exhibition of new forces, but the outcome 221of a special combination of old. Mental facts are therefore essentially dependent on molecular facts; molecular facts are not dependent on mental. They may seem to be so, but this is only seeming. They are as much the outcome of molecular groupings and movements as the figures in a kaleidoscope are of the groupings and movements of the colored bits of glass. They are things entirely by the way; and they can as little be considered links in any chain of causes as can the figure in a kaleidoscope be called the cause of the figure that succeeds it.

The conclusion, however, is so distasteful to most men, that but few of them can be brought even to face it, still less to accept it. There is not a single physicist of eminence— none at least who has spoken publicly on the moral aspects of life—who has honestly and fairly considered it, and said plainly whether he accepts it, rejects it, or is in doubt about it. On the contrary, instead of meeting this question, they all do their best to avoid it, and to hide it from themselves and others in a vague haze of mystery. And there is a peculiarity in the nature of the subject that has made this task an easy one. But the dust they have raised is not impenetrable, and can, with a little patience, be laid altogether.

The phenomenon of consciousness is in one way unique. It is the only phenomenon with which science comes in contact, of which the scientific imagination cannot form a coherent picture. It has a side, it is true, that we can picture well enough—'the thrilling of the nerves,' as Dr. Tyndall says, 'the discharging of the muscles, and all the subsequent changes of the organism.' But of how these changes come to have another side, we can form no picture. This, it is perfectly true, is a complete mystery. And this mystery it is that our modern physicists seize on, and try to hide and lose in the shadow of it a conclusion which they admit that, in any other case, a rigorous logic would force on them.

The following is a typical example of the way in which they do this. It is taken from Dr. Tyndall. 'The mechanical philosopher, as such,' he says, 'will never place a state of consciousness and a group of molecules in the position of mover and moved. Observation proves them to interact; but in passing from one to the other, we meet a blank which the logic of deduction is unable to fill.... I lay bare unsparingly the initial difficulty of the materialist, and tell him that the facts of observation which he considers so simple are "almost as difficult to be seized as the idea of a soul." I go further, and say in effect: "If you abandon the interpretation of grosser minds, who image the soul as a Psyche which could be thrown out of the window—an entity which is usually occupied we know not how, among the molecules of the brain, but which on due occasion, such as the intrusion of a bullet, or the blow of a club, can fly away into other regions of space—if abandoning this heathen notion you approach the subject in the only way in which approach is possible—if you consent to make your soul a poetic rendering of a phenomenon which—as I have taken more pains than anyone else to show you—refuses the ordinary yoke of physical laws, then I, for one, would not object to this exercise of ideality." I say it strongly, but with good temper, that the theologian who hacks and scourges me for putting the matter in this light is guilty of black ingratitude.'

Now if we examine this very typical passage, we shall see that in it are confused two questions which, as regards our own relation to them, are on a totally different footing. One of these questions cannot be answered at all. The other can be answered in distinct and opposite ways. About the one we must rest in wonder; about the other we must make a choice. And the feat which our modern physicists are trying to perform is to hide the importunate nature of the second in the dark folds of the first. This first question is, Why should consciousness be connected with the brain at all? The second question is, What is it when connected? Is it simply the product of the brain's movement; or is the brain's movement in any degree produced by it? We only know it, so to speak, as the noise made by the working of the brain's machinery—as the crash, the roar, or the whisper of its restless colliding molecules. Is this machinery self-moving, or is it, at least, modulated, if not moved, by some force other than itself? The brain is the organ of consciousness, just as the instrument called an organ is an organ of music; and consciousness itself is as a tune emerging from the organ-pipes. Expressed in terms of this metaphor our two questions are as follows. The first is, Why, when the air goes through them, are the organ-pipes resonant? The second is, What controls the mechanism by which the air is regulated—a musician, or a revolving barrel? Now what our modern physicists fail to see is, not only that these two questions are distinct in detail, but that also they are distinct in kind; that a want of power to answer them means, in the two cases, not a distinct thing only, but also an opposite thing; and that our confessed impotence to form any conjecture at all as to the first, does not in the least exonerate us from choosing between conjectures as to the second.

As to the first question, our discovery of the fact it is concerned with, and our utter inability to account for this fact, has really no bearing at all upon the great dilemma—the dilemma as to the unity or the dualism of existence, and the independence or automatism of the life and will of man. All that science tells us on this first head the whole world may agree with, with the utmost readiness; and if any theologian 'hacks and scourges' Dr. Tyndall for his views thus far, he must, beyond all doubt, be a very foolish theologian indeed. The whole bearing of this matter modern science seems to confuse and magnify, and it fancies itself assaulted by opponents who in reality have no existence. Let a man be never so theological, and never so pledged to a faith in myths and mysteries, he would not have the least interest in denying that the brain, though we know not how, is the only seat for us of thought and mind and spirit. Let him have never so firm a faith in life immortal, yet this immortal has, he knows, put on mortality, through an inexplicable contact with matter; and his faith is not in the least shaken by learning that this point of contact is the brain. He can admit with the utmost readiness that the brain is the only instrument through which supernatural life is made at the same time natural life. He can admit that the moral state of a saint might be detected by some form of spectroscope. At first sight, doubtless, this may appear somewhat startling; but there is nothing really in it that is either strange or formidable. Dr. Tyndall says that the view indicated can, 'he thinks,' be maintained 'against all attack.' But why he should apprehend any attack at all, and why he should only 'think' it would be unsuccessful, it is somewhat hard to conceive. To say that a spectroscope as applied to the brain might conceivably detect such a thing as sanctity, is little more than to say that our eyes as applied to the face can actually detect such a thing as anger. There is nothing in that doctrine to alarm the most mystical of believers. In the completeness with which it is now brought before us it is doubtless new and wonderful, and will doubtless tend presently to clarify human thought. But no one need fear to accept it as a truth; and probably before long we shall all accept it as a truism. It is not denying the existence of a soul to say that it cannot move in matter without leaving some impress in matter, any more than it is denying the existence of an organist to say that he cannot play to us without striking the notes of his organ. Dr. Tyndall then need hardly have used so much emphasis and iteration in affirming that 'every thought and feeling has its definite mechanical correlative, that it is accompanied by a certain breaking-up and re-marshalling of the atoms of the brain.' And he is no more likely to be 'hacked and scourged' for doing so than he would be for affirming that every note we hear in a piece of music has its definite correlative in the mechanics of the organ, and that it is accompanied by a depression and a rising again of some particular key. In his views thus far the whole world may agree with him; whilst when he adds so emphatically that in these views there is still involved a mystery, we shall not so much say that the world agrees with him as that he, like a good sensible man, agrees with the world. The passage from mind to matter is, Dr. Tyndall says, unthinkable. The common sense of mankind has always said the same. We have here a something, not which we are doubtful how to explain, but which we cannot explain at all. We have not to choose or halt between alternative conjectures, for there are absolutely no conjectures to halt between. We are now, as to this point, in the same state of mind in which we have always been, only this state of mind has been revealed to us more clearly. We are in theoretical ignorance, but we are in no practical perplexity.

The perplexity comes in with the second question; and it is here that the issue lies between the affirmation and the denial of a second and a supernatural order. We will see, first, how this question is put and treated by Dr. Tyndall, and we will then see what his treatment comes to. Is it true, he asks, as many physicists hold it is, 'that the physical processes are complete in themselves, and would go on just as they do if consciousness were not at all implicated,' as an engine might go on working though it made no noise, or as a barrel-organ might go on playing even though there were no ear to listen to it? Or do 'states of consciousness enter as links into the chain of antecedence and sequence which gives rise to bodily actions?' Such is the question in Dr. Tyndall's own phrases; and here, in his own phrases also, comes his answer. 'I have no power,' he says, 'of imagining such states interposed between the molecules of the brain, and influencing the transference of motion among the molecules. The thing eludes all mental presentation. But,' he adds, 'the production of consciousness by molecular motion is quite as unpresentable to the mental vision as the production of molecular motion by consciousness. If I reject one result, I reject both. I, however, reject neither, and thus stand in the presence of two Incomprehensibles, instead of one Incomprehensible.'

Now what does all this mean? There is one meaning of which the words are capable, which would make them perfectly clear and coherent; but that meaning, as we shall see presently, cannot possibly be Dr. Tyndall's. They would be perfectly clear and coherent if he meant this by them—that the brain was a natural instrument, in the hands of a supernatural player; but that why the instrument should be able to be played upon, and how the player should be able to play upon it, were both matters on which he could throw no light. But elsewhere he has told us expressly that he does not mean this. This he expressly says is 'the interpretation229 of grosser minds,' and science will not for a moment permit us to retain it. The brain contains no 'entity usually occupied we know not how amongst its molecules,' but at the same time separable from them. According to him, this is a 'heathen' notion, and, until we abandon it, 'no approach,' he says, 'to the subject is possible.' What does he mean, then, when he tells us he rejects neither result; when he tells us that he believes that molecular motion produces consciousness, and also that consciousness in its turn produces molecular motion?—when he tells us distinctly of these two that 'observation proves them to interact'? If such language as this means anything, it must have reference to two distinct forces, one material and the other immaterial. Indeed, does he not himself say so? Does he not tell us that one of the beliefs he does not reject is the belief in 'states of consciousness interposed between the molecules of the brain, and influencing the transference of motion among the molecules'? It is perfectly clear, then, that these states are not molecules; in other words, they are not material. But if not material, what are they, acting on matter, and yet distinct from matter? What can they belong to but that 'heathen' thing the soul—that 'entity which could be thrown out of the window,' and which, as Dr. Tyndall has said elsewhere, science forbids us to believe in? Surely 230for an exact thinker this is thought in strange confusion. 'Matter,' he says, 'I define as that mysterious something by which all this is accomplished;' and yet here we find him, in the face of this, invoking some second mystery as well. And for what reason? This is the strangest thing of all. He believes in his second Incomprehensible because he believes in his first Incomprehensible. 'If I reject one result,' he says, 'I must reject both. I, however, reject neither.' But why? Because one undoubted fact is a mystery, is every mystery an undoubted fact? Such is Dr. Tyndall's logic in this remarkable utterance: and if this logic be valid, we can at once prove to him the existence of a personal God, and a variety of other 'heathen' doctrines also. But, applied in this way, it is evident that the argument fails to move him; for a belief in a personal God is one of the first things that his science rejects. What shall we say of him, then, when he applies the argument in his own way? We can say simply this—that his mind for the time being is in a state of such confusion, that he is incapable really of clearly meaning anything. What his position logically must be—what, on other occasions, he clearly avows it to be—is plain enough. It is essentially that of a man confronted by one Incomprehensible, not confronted by two. But, looked at in certain ways, or rather looked from in certain ways, this position 231seems to stagger him. The problem of existence reels and grows dim before him, and he fancies that he detects the presence of two Incomprehensibles, when he has really, in his state of mental insobriety, only seen one Incomprehensible double. If this be not the case, it must be one that, intellectually, is even weaker than this. It must be that, not of a man with a single coherent theory which his intellect in its less vigorous moments sometimes relaxes its hold upon, but it must be that of a man with two hostile theories which he vainly imagines to be one, and which he inculcates alternately, each with an equal emphasis.

If this bewilderment were peculiar to Dr. Tyndall, I should have no motive or meaning in thus dwelling on it. But it is no peculiarity of his. It is characteristic of the whole school he belongs to; it is inherent in our whole modern positivism—the whole of our exact and enlightened thought. I merely choose Dr. Tyndall as my example, not because there is more confusion in his mind than there is in that of his fellow-physicists, but because he is, as it were, the enfant terrible of his family, who publicly lets out the secrets which the others are more careful to conceal.

But I have not done with this matter yet. We are here dealing with the central problem of things, and we must not leave it till we have made it as plain as possible. I will therefore re-state it in terms of another metaphor. Let us compare the universal matter, with its infinity of molecules, to a number of balls on a billiard-table, set in motion by the violent stroke of a cue. The balls at once begin to strike each other and rebound from the cushions at all angles and in all directions, and assume with regard to each other positions of every kind. At last six of them collide or cannon in a particular corner of the table, and thus group themselves so as to form a human brain; and their various changes thereafter, so long as the brain remains a brain, represent the various changes attendant on a man's conscious life. Now in this life let us take some moral crisis. Let us suppose the low desire to cling to some pleasing or comforting superstition is contending with the heroic desire to face the naked truth at all costs. The man in question is at first about to yield to the low desire. For a time there is a painful struggle in him. At last there is a sharp decisive pang; the heroic desire is the conqueror, the superstition is cast away, and 'though truth slay me,' says the man, 'yet will I trust in it.' Such is the aspect of the question when approached from one side. But what is it when approached from the other? The six billiard balls have simply changed their places. When they corresponded to low desire, they formed, let us say, an oval; when they corresponded to the heroic desire, they formed, let us say, a circle. Now what is the cause and what the conditions of this change? Clearly a certain impetus imparted to the balls, and certain fixed laws under which that impetus operates. The question is what laws and what impetus are these? Are they the same or not the same, now the balls correspond to consciousness, as they were before, when the balls did not correspond to it? One of two things must happen. Either the balls go on moving by exactly the same laws and forces they have always moved by, and are in the grasp of the same invincible necessity, or else there is some new and disturbing force in the midst of them, with which we have to reckon. But if consciousness is inseparable from matter, this cannot be. Do the billiard-balls when so grouped as to represent consciousness generate some second motive power distinct from, at variance with, and often stronger than, the original impetus? Clearly no scientific thinker can admit this. To do so would be to undermine the entire fabric of science, to contradict what is its first axiom and its last conclusion. If then the motion of our six billiard balls has anything, when it corresponds to consciousness, distinct in kind from what it always had, it can only derive this from one cause. That cause is a second cue, tampering with the balls and interfering with them, or even more than this—a second hand taking them up and arranging them arbitrarily in certain figures.

Science places the positive school on the horns of a dilemma. The mind or spirit is either arranged entirely by the molecules it is connected with, and these molecules move with the same automatic necessity that the earth moves with; or else these molecules are, partially at least, arranged by the mind or spirit. If we do not accept the former theory we must accept the latter: there is no third course open to us. If man is not an automaton, his consciousness is no mere function of any physical organ. It is an alien and disturbing element. Its impress on physical facts, its disturbance of physical laws, may be doubtless the only things through which we can perceive its existence; but it is as distinct from the things by which we can alone at present perceive it, as a hand unseen in the dark, that should arrest or change the course of a phosphorescent billiard-ball. Once let us deny even in the most qualified way that the mind in the most absolute way is a material machine, an automaton, and in that denial we are affirming a second and immaterial universe, independent of the material, and obeying different laws. But of this universe, if it exists, no natural proof can be given, because ex hypothesi it lies quite beyond the region of nature.

One theory then of man's life is that it is a union of two orders of things; another, that it is single, and belongs to only one. And of these theories—opposite, and mutually exclusive, Dr. Tyndall, and modern positivism with him, says 'I reject neither.'

Now this statement of their position, if taken as they state it, is of course nonsense. It is impossible to consider matter as 'that mysterious something by which all that is is accomplished;' and then to solve the one chief riddle of things by a second mysterious something that is not material. Nor can we 'reject,' as the positivists say they do, an 'outside builder' of the world, and then claim the assistance of an outside orderer of the brain. The positivists would probably tell us that they do not do so, or that they do not mean to do so. And we may well believe them. Their fault is that they do not know what they mean. I will try to show them.

First, they mean something, with which, as I have said already, we may all agree. They mean that matter moving under certain laws (which may possibly be part and parcel of its own essence) combines after many changes into the human brain, every motion of which has its definite connection with consciousness, and its definite correspondence to some state of it. And this fact is a mystery, though it may be questioned if it be more mysterious why matter should think of itself, than why it should move of itself. At any rate, thus far we are all agreed; and whatever mystery we may be dealing with, it is one that leaves us in ignorance but not in doubt. The doubt comes in at the next step. We have then not to wonder at one fact, but, the mystery being in either case the same, to choose between two hypotheses. The first is that there is in consciousness one order of forces only, the second is that there are two. And when the positive school say that they reject neither of these, what they really mean to say is that as to the second they neither dare openly do one thing or the other—to deny it or accept it, but that they remain like an awkward child when offered some more pudding, blushing and looking down, and utterly unable to say either yes or no.

Now the question to ask the positive school is this. Why are they in this state of suspense? 'There is an iron strength in the logic,' as Dr. Tyndall himself says, that rejects the second order altogether. The hypothesis of its existence explains no fact of observation. The scheme of nature, if it cannot be wholly explained without it, can, at any rate, be explained better without it than with it. Indeed from the standpoint of the thinker who holds that all that is is matter, it seems a thing too superfluous, too unmeaning, to be even worth denial. And yet the positive school announce solemnly that they will not deny it. Now why is this? It is true that they cannot prove its non-existence; but this is no reason for professing a solemn uncertainty as to its existence. We cannot prove that each time a cab drives down Regent Street a stick of barley-sugar is not created in Sirius. But we do not proclaim, to the world our eternal ignorance as to whether or no this is so. Why then should our positivists treat in this way the alleged immaterial part of consciousness? Why this emphatic protestation on their part that there may exist a something which, as far as the needs of their science go, is superfluous, and as far as the logic of their science goes is impossible? The answer is plain. Though their science does not need it, the moral value of life does. As to that value they have certain foregone conclusions, which they cannot resolve to abandon, but which their science can make no room for. Two alternatives are offered them—to admit that life has not the meaning they thought it had, or that their system has not the completeness they thought it had; and of these two alternatives they will accept neither. They could tell us 'with an iron strength of logic' that all human sorrow was as involuntary and as unmeaning as sea-sickness; that love and faith were but distillations of what exists diluted in mutton-chops and beer; and that the voice of one crying in the wilderness was nothing but an automatic metamorphosis of the locusts and wild honey. They could tell us 'with an iron strength of logic' that all the thoughts and moral struggles of humanity were but as the clanging whirr of a machine, which if a little better adjusted might for the future go on spinning in silence. But they see that the discovery on man's part that his life was nothing more than this would mean a complete change in its mechanism, and that thenceforward its entire action would be different. They therefore seek a refuge in saying it may be more than this. But what do they mean by may be? Do they mean that in spite of all that science can teach them, in spite of that uniformity absolute and omnipresent which alone it reveals to them, which day by day it is forcing with more vividness on their imaginations, and which seems to have no room for anything besides itself—do they mean that in spite of this there may still be a second something, a power of a different order, acting on man's brain and grappling with its automatic movements? Do they mean that that 'heathen' and 'gross' conception of an immaterial soul is probably after all the true one? Either they must mean this or else they must mean the exact opposite. There is no third course open to them.36

Their opinion, as soon as they form one, must rest either on this extreme or that. They will see, as exact and scientific thinkers, that if it be not practically certain that there is some supernatural entity in us, it is practically certain that there is not one. To say merely that it may exist is but to put an ounce in one scale whilst there is a ton in the other. It is an admission that is utterly dead and meaningless. They can only entertain the question of its existence because its existence is essential to man as a moral being. The only reason that can tempt us to say it may be forces us in the same moment to say that it must be, and that it is.

Which answer eventually the positive school will choose, and which answer men in general will accept, I make as I have said before, no attempt to answer. My only purpose to show is, that if man has any moral being at all, he has it in virtue of his immaterial will—a force, a something of which physical science can give no account whatever, and which it has no shadow of authority either for affirming or for denying; and further, that if we are not prevented by it from affirming his immaterial will, we are not prevented from affirming his immortality, and the existence of God likewise.

And now I come to that third point which I said I should deal with here, but which I have not yet touched upon. Every logical reasoner who admits the power of will must admit not only the possibility of miracles, but also the actual fact of their daily and hourly occurrence. Every exertion of the human will is a miracle in the strictest sense of the word; only it takes place privately, within the closed walls of the brain. The molecules of the brain are arranged and ordered by a supernatural agency. Their natural automatic movements are suspended, or directed and interfered with. It is true that in common usage the word miracle has a more restricted sense. It is applied generally not to the action of man's will, but of God's. But the sense in both cases is essentially the same. God's will is conceived of as disturbing the automatic movements of matter without the skull, in just the same way as man's will is conceived of as disturbing those of the brain within it. Nor, though the alleged manifestations of the former do more violence to the scientific imagination than do those of the latter, are they in the eye of reason one whit more impossible. The erection of a pyramid at the will of an Egyptian king would as much disturb the course of nature as the removal of a mountain by the faith of a Galilean fisherman; whilst the flooding of the Sahara at the will of a speculating company would interfere with the weather of Europe far more than the most believing of men ever thought that any answer to prayer would.

It will thus be seen that morality and religion are, so far as science goes, on one and the same footing—of one and the same substance, and that as assailed by science they either fall together or stand together. It will be seen too that the power of science against them resides not in itself, but in a certain intellectual fulcrum that we ourselves supply it with. That its methods can discover no trace of either of them, of itself proves nothing, unless we first lay down as a dogma that its methods of discovery are the only methods. If we are prepared to abide by this, there is little more to be said. The rest, it is becoming daily plainer, is a very simple process; and what we have to urge against religion will thenceforth amount to this. There is no supernatural, because everything is natural; there is no spirit, because everything is matter; or there is no air, because everything is earth; there is no fire, because everything is water; a rose has no smell because our eyes cannot detect any.

This, in its simplest form, is the so-called argument of modern materialism. Argument, however, it is quite plain it is not. It is a mere dogmatic statement, that can give no logical account of itself, and must trust, for its acceptance, to the world's vague sense of its fitness. The modern world, it is true, has mistaken it for an argument, and has been cowed by it accordingly; but the mistake is a simple one, and can be readily accounted for. The dogmatism of denial was formerly a sort of crude rebellion, inconsistent with itself, and vulnerable in a thousand places. Nature, as then known, was, to all who could weigh the wonder of it, a thing inexplicable without some supernatural agency. Indeed, marks of such an agency seemed to meet men everywhere. But now all this has changed. Step by step science has been unravelling the tangle, and has loosened with its human fingers the knots that once seemed deo digni vindice. It has enabled us to see in nature a complete machine, needing no aid from without. It has made a conception of things rational and coherent that was formerly absurd and arbitrary. Science has done all this; but this is all that it has done. The dogmatism of denial it has left as it found it, an unverified and unverifiable assertion. It has simply made this dogmatism consistent with itself. But in doing this, as men will soon come to see, it has done a great deal more than its chief masters bargained for. Nature, as explained by science, is nothing more than a vast automaton; and man with all his ways and works is simply a part of Nature, and can, by no device of thought, be detached from or set above it. He is as absolutely automatic as a tree is, or as a flower is; and is an incapable as a tree or flower of any spiritual responsibility or significance. Here we see the real limits of science. It will explain the facts of life to us, it is true, but it will not explain the value that hitherto we have attached to them. Is that solemn value a fact or fancy? As far as proof and reason go, we can answer either way. We have two simple and opposite statements set against each other, between which argument will give us no help in choosing, and between which the only arbiter is a judgment formed upon utterly alien grounds. As for proof, the nature of the case does not admit of it. The world of moral facts, if it existed a thousand times, could give no more proof of its existence than it does now. If on other grounds we believe that it does exist, then signs, if not proofs of it, at once surround us everywhere. But let the belief in its reality fail us, and instantly the whole cloud of witnesses vanishes. For science to demand a proof that shall convince it on its own premises is to demand an impossibility, and to involve a contradiction in terms. Science is only possible on the assumption that nature is uniform. Morality is only possible on the assumption that this uniformity is interfered with by the will. The world of morals is as distinct from the world of science as a wine is from the cup that holds it; and to say that it does not exist because science can find no trace of it, is to say that a bird has not flown over a desert because it has left no footprints in the sand. And as with morals, so it is with religion. Science will allow us to deny or to affirm both. Reason will not allow us to deny or affirm only one.

[33] The argument has been used in this exact form by Professor Clifford.

[34] Dreams and Realities, by Leslie Stephen.

[35] The feebleness and vacillation of Dr. Tyndall's whole views of things, as soon as they bear on matters that are of any universal moment, is so typical of the entire positive thought of the day, that I may with advantage give one or two further illustrations of it. Although in one place he proclaims loudly that the emergence of consciousness from matter must ever remain a mystery, he yet shows indication of a hope that it may yet be solved. He quotes with approval, and with an implication that he himself leans to the view expressed in them, the following words of Ueberweg, whom he calls 'one of the subtlest heads that Germany has produced.' 'What happens in the brain, says Ueberweg, 'would in my opinion not be possible if the process which here appears in its greatest concentration, did not obtain generally, only in a vastly diminished degree. Take a pair of mice, and a cask of flour. By copious nourishment the animals increase and multiply, and in the same proportion sensations and feelings augment. The quantity of these preserved by the first pair is not simply diffused among their descendants, for in that case the last would feel more fully than the first. The sensations and the feelings must necessarily be referred back to the flour, where they exist, weak and pale, it is true, and not concentrated, as in the brain.' 'We may not,' Dr. Tyndall adds, by way of a gloss to this, 'be able to taste or smell alcohol in a tub of fermented cherries, but by distillation we obtain from them concentrated Kirschwasser. Hence Ueberweg's comparison of the brain to a still, which concentrates the sensation and feeling pre-existing, but diluted, in the food.'

Let us now compare this with the following. 'It is no explanation,' says Dr. Tyndall, 'to say that objective and subjective are two sides of one and the same phenomenon. Why should phenomena have two sides? There are plenty of molecular motions which do not exhibit this two-sidedness. Does water think or feel when it runs into frost-ferns upon a window pane? If not, why should the molecular motions of the brain be yoked to this mysterious companion consciousness?'

Here we have two views, diametrically opposed to each other, the one suggested with approval, and the other implied as his own, by the same writer, and in the same short essay. The first view is that consciousness is the general property of all matter, just as motion is. The second view is that consciousness is not the general property of matter, but the inexplicable property of the brain only.

Here again we have a similar inconsistency. Upon one page Dr. Tyndall says that when we have 'exhausted physics, and reached its very rim, a mighty Mystery stills looms beyond us. We have made no step towards its solution. And thus it will ever loom.' And on the opposite page he says thus: 'If asked whether science has solved, or is likely in our day to solve, the problem of the universe, I must shake my head in doubt.'

Further, I will remind the reader of Dr. Tyndall's arguments, on one occasion, against any outside builder or creator of the material universe. He argued that such did not exist, because his supposed action was not definitely presentable. 'I should enquire after its shape,' he says:—'Has it legs or arms? If not, I would wish it to be made clear to me how a thing without these appliances can act so perfectly the part of a builder? He challenged the theist (the theist addressed at the time was Dr. Martineau) to give him some account of his God's workings; and 'When he does this,' said Dr. Tyndall, 'I shall "demand of him an immediate exercise" of the power "of definite mental presentation."' If he fails here, Dr. Tyndall argues, his case is at once disproved; for nothing exists that is not thus presentable. Let us compare this with his dealing with the fact of consciousness. Consciousness, he admits, is not thus presentable; and yet consciousness, he admits, exists.

Instances might be multiplied of the same vacillation and confusion of thought—the same feminine inability to be constant to one train of reasoning. But those just given suffice. What weight can we attach to a man's philosophy, who after telling us that consciousness may possibly be an inherent property of matter, of which 'the receit of reason is a limbec only,' adds in the same breath almost, that matter generally is certainly not conscious, and that consciousness comes to the brain we know not whence nor wherefore? What shall we say of a man who in one sentence tells us that it is impossible that science can ever solve the riddle of things, and tells us in the next sentence that it is doubtful if this impossibility will be accomplished within the next fifty years?—who argues that God is a mystery, and therefore God is a fiction; who admits that consciousness is a fact, and yet proclaims that it is a mystery; and who says that the fact of matter producing consciousness being a mystery, proves the mystery of consciousness acting on matter to be a fact?

[36] It is true that one of the favourite teachings of the positive school is, that as to this question the proper attitude is that of Agnosticism; in other words, that a state of perpetual suspense on this subject is the only rational one. They are asked, have we a soul, a will, and consequently any moral responsibility? And the answer is that they must shake their heads in doubt. It is true they tell us that it is but as men of science that they shake their heads. But Dr. Tyndall tells us what this admission means. 'If the materialist is confounded,' he says, 'and science rendered dumb, who else is prepared with an answer? Let us lower our heads and acknowledge our ignorance, priest and philosopher—one and all.' In like manner, referring to the feeling which others have supposed to be a sense of God's presence and majesty: this, for the 'man of science,' he says is the sense of a 'power which gives fulness and force, to his existence, but which he can neither analyse nor comprehend.' Which means, that because a physical specialist cannot analyse this sense, it is therefore incapable of analysis. A bishop might with equal propriety use just the same language about a glass of port wine, and argue with, equal cogency that it was a primary and simple element. What is meant is, that the facts of the materialist are the only facts we can be certain of; and because these can give man no moral guidance, that therefore man can have no moral guidance at all.

Let us illustrate the case by some example that is mentally presentable. Some ruined girl, we will say, oppressed with a sense of degradation, comes to Dr. Tyndall and lays her case before him. 'I have heard you are a very wise man,' she says to him, 'and that you have proved that the priest is all wrong, who prepared me a year ago for my confirmation. Now tell me, I beseech you tell me, is mine really the desperate state I have been taught to think it is? May my body be likened to the temple of the Holy Ghost defiled? or do I owe it no more reverence than I owe the Alhambra Theatre? Am I guilty, and must I seek repentance? or am I not guilty, and may I go on just as I please?' 'My dear girl,' Dr. Tyndall replies to her, 'I must shake my head in doubt. Come, let its lower our heads, and acknowledge our ignorance as to whether you are a wretched girl or no. Materialism is confounded, and science rendered dumb by questions such as yours; they can, therefore, never be answered, and must always remain open. I may add, however, that if you ask me personally whether I consider you to be degraded, I lean to the affirmative. But I can give you no reason in support of this judgment, so you may attach to it what value you will.'

Such is the position of agnostics, when brought face to face with the world. They are undecided only about one question, and this is the one question which cannot be left undecided. Men cannot remain agnostics as to belief that their actions must depend upon, any more than a man who is compelled to go on walking can refrain from choosing one road or other when there are two open to him. Nor does it matter that our believing may in neither case amount to a complete certitude. It is sufficient that the balance of probability be on one side or the other. Two ounces will out-weigh one ounce, quite as surely as a ton will. But what our philosophers profess to teach us (in so far as they profess to be agnostics, and disclaim being dogmatists) is, that there is no balance either way. The message they shout to us is, that they have no message at all; and that because they are without one, the whole world is in the same condition.

Is Life Worth Living? By William Hurrell Mallock

CHAPTER X.

MORALITY AND NATURAL THEISM.

Credo quia impossibile est.

If we look calmly at the possible future of human thought, it will appear from what we have just seen, that physical science of itself can do little to control or cramp it; nor until man consents to resign his belief in virtue and his own dignity altogether, will it be able to repress religious faith, should other causes tend to produce a new outbreak of it. But the chief difficulties in the matter are still in store for us. Let us see never so clearly that science, if we are moral beings, can do nothing to weaken our belief in God and immortality, but still leaves us free, if we will, to believe in them, it seems getting clearer and yet more clear that these beliefs are inconsistent with themselves, and conflict with these very moral feelings, of which they are invoked as an explanation. Here it is true that reason does confront us, and what answer to make to it is a very serious question. This applies even to natural religion in its haziest and most compliant form; and as applied to any form of orthodoxy its force is doubled. What we have seen thus far is, that if there be a moral world at all, our knowledge of nature contains nothing inconsistent with theism. We have now to enquire how far theism is inconsistent with our conceptions of the moral world.

In treating these difficulties, we will for the present consider them as applying only to religion in general, not to any special form of it. The position of orthodoxy we will reserve for a separate treatment. For convenience' sake, however, I shall take as a symbol of all religion the vaguer and more general teachings of Christianity; but I shall be adducing them not as teachings revealed by heaven, but simply as developed by the religious consciousness of men.

To begin then with the great primary difficulties: these, though they take various forms, can all in the last resort be reduced to two—the existence of evil in the face of the power of God, and the freedom of man's will in the face of the will of God. And what I shall try to make plain with respect to these is this: not that they are not difficulties—not that they are not insoluble difficulties; but that they are not difficulties due to religion or theism, nor by abandoning theism can we in any way escape from them. They start into being not with the belief in God, and a future of rewards and punishments, but with the belief in the moral law and in virtue, and they are common to all systems in which the worth of virtue is recognised.

The vulgar view of the matter cannot be better stated than in the following account given by J. S. Mill of the anti-religious reasonings of his father. He looked upon religion, says his son, 'as the greatest enemy of morality; first, by setting up fictitious excellences—belief in creeds, devotional feelings, and ceremonies, not connected with the good of humankind, and causing them to be accepted as substitutes for genuine virtues; but above all by radically vitiating the standard of morals, making it consist in doing the will of a being, on whom, indeed, it lavishes all the phrases of adulation, but whom, in sober truth, it depicts as eminently hateful. I have a hundred times heard him say that all ages and nations have represented their gods as wicked in a constantly increasing progression; that mankind had gone on adding trait after trait, till they reached the most perfect expression of wickedness which the human mind can devise, and have called this God, and prostrated themselves before it. The ne plus ultra of wickedness he considered to be embodied in what is commonly presented to mankind as the creed of Christianity. Think (he used to say) of a being who would make a hell—who would create the human race with the infallible foreknowledge, and therefore with the intention, that the great majority of them, should be consigned to horrible and everlasting torment.' James Mill, adds his son, knew quite well that Christians were not, in fact, as demoralised by this monstrous creed as, if they were logically consistent, they ought to be. 'The same slovenliness of thought (he said) and subjection of the reason to fears, wishes, and affections, which enable them to accept a theory involving a contradiction in terms, prevent them from perceiving the logical consequence of the theory.'

Now, in spite of its coarse and exaggerated acrimony, this passage doubtless expresses a great truth, which presently I shall go on to consider. But it contains also a very characteristic falsehood, of which we must first divest it. God is here represented as making a hell, with the express intention of forcibly putting men into it, and His main hatefulness consists in this capricious and wanton cruelty. Such a representation is, however, an essentially false one. It is not only not true to the true Christian teaching, but it is absolutely opposed to it. The God of Christianity does not make hell; still less does He deliberately put men into it. It is made by men themselves; the essence of its torment consists in the loss of God; and those that lose Him, lose Him by their own act, from having deliberately made themselves incapable of loving Him. God never wills the death of the sinner. It is to the sinner's own will that the sinner's death is due.

All this rhetoric, therefore, about God's malevolence and wickedness is entirely beside the point, nor does it even touch the difficulty that, in his heart, James Mill is aiming at. His main difficulty is nothing more than this: How can an infinite will that rules everywhere, find room for a finite will not in harmony with itself? Whilst the only farther perplexity that the passage indicates, is the existence of those evil conditions by which the finite will, already so weak and wavering, is yet farther hampered.

Now these difficulties are doubtless quite as great as James Mill thought they were; but we must observe this, that they are not of the same kind. They are merely intellectual difficulties. They are not moral difficulties at all. Mill truly says that they involve a contradiction in terms. But why? Not, as Mill says, because a wicked God is set up as the object of moral worship, but because, in spite of all the wickedness existing, the Author of all existences is affirmed not to be wicked.

Nor, again, is Mill right in saying that this contradiction is due to 'slovenliness of thought.' Theology accepts it with its eyes wide open, making no attempt to explain the inexplicable; and the human will it treats in the same way. It makes no offer to us to clear up everything, or to enable thought to put a girdle round the universe. On the contrary, it proclaims with emphasis that its first axioms are 252unthinkable; and its most renowned philosophic motto is, 'I believe because it is impossible.'

What shall it say, then, when assailed by the rational moralist? It will not deny its own condition, but it will show its opponent that his is really the same. It will show him that, let him give his morality what base he will, he cannot conceive of things without the same contradiction in terms. If good be a thing of any spiritual value—if it be, in other words, what every moral system supposes it to be—that good can co-exist with evil is just as unthinkable as that God can. The value of moral good is supposed to lie in this—that by it we are put en rapport with something that is better than ourselves—some 'stream of tendency,' let us say, 'that makes for righteousness,' But if this stream of tendency be not a personal God, what is it? Is it Nature? Nature, we have seen already, is open to just the same objections that God is. It is equally guilty of all the evil that is contained in it. Is it Truth, then—pure Truth for its own sake? Again, we have seen already that as little can it be that. Is it Human Nature as opposed to Nature?—Man as distinct from, and holier than, any individual men? Of all the substitutes for God this at first sight seems the most promising, or, at any rate, the most practical. But, apart from all the other objections to this, which we have already been considering in such detail, it 253will very soon be apparent that it involves the very same inconsistency, the same contradiction in terms. The fact of moral evil still confronts us, and the humanity to which we lift our hearts up is still taxable with that. But perhaps we separate the good in humanity from the evil, and only worship the former as struggling to get free from the latter. This, however, will be of little help to us. If what we call humanity is nothing but the good part of it, we can only vindicate its goodness at the expense of its strength. Evil is at least an equal match for it, and in most of the battles hitherto it is evil that has been victorious. But to conceive of good in this way is really to destroy our conception of it. Goodness is in itself an incomplete notion; it is but one facet of a figure which, approached from other sides, appears to us as eternity, as omnipresence, and, above all, as supreme strength; and to reduce goodness to nothing but the higher part of humanity—to make it a wavering fitful flame that continually sinks and flickers, that at its best can but blaze for a while, and at its brightest can throw no light beyond this paltry parish of a world—is to deprive it of its whole meaning and hold on us. Or again, even were this not so, and could we believe, and be strengthened by believing, that the good in humanity would one day gain the victory, and that some higher future, which even we might partake in by preparing, was in store for the human race, would our conception of the matter then be any more harmonious? As we surveyed our race as a whole, would its brighter future ever do away with its past? Would not the depth and the darkness of the shadow grow more portentous as the light grew brighter? And would not man's history strike more clearly on us as the ghastly embodiment of a vast injustice? But it may be said that the sorrows of the past will hereafter be dead and done with; that evil will literally be as though it had never been. Well, and so in a short time will the good likewise; and if we are ever to think lightly of the world's sinful and sorrowful past, we shall have to think equally lightly of its sinless and cheerful future.

Let us pass now to the secondary points. Opponents of theism, or of religion in general, are perpetually attacking it for its theories of a future life. Its eternal rewards and punishments are to them permanent stumbling-blocks. A future life of happiness they think an unmeaning promise; and a future life of misery they think an unworthy and brutal threat. And if reason and observation are to be our only guides, we cannot say that they do not argue with justice. If we believe in heaven, we believe in something that the imagination fails to grasp. If we believe in hell, we believe in something that our moral sense revolts at: for though hell may be nothing but the conscious loss of God, and though those that lose Him may have made their own hell for themselves, still their loss, if eternal, will be an eternal flaw and disease in the sum of things—the eternal self-assertion against omnipotence of some depraved and alien power.

From these difficulties it is impossible to escape. All we can do here, as in the former case, is to show that they are not peculiar to the special doctrines to which they are supposed generally to be due; but that they are equally inseparable from any of the proposed substitutes. We can only show that they are inevitable, not that they are not insoluble. If we condemn a belief in heaven because it is unthinkable, we must for the same reason, as we have seen already, condemn a Utopia on earth—the thing we are now told we should fix our hopes upon, instead of it. As to the second question—that of eternal punishment, we may certainly here get rid of one difficulty by adopting the doctrine of a final restitution. But, though one difficulty will be thus got rid of, another equally great will take its place. Our moral sense, it is true, will no more be shocked by the conception of an eternal discord in things, but we shall be confronted by a fatalism that will allow to us no moral being at all. If we shall all reach the same place in the end—if inevitably we shall all do so—it is quite plain that our freedom to choose in the matter is a freedom that is apparent only. Mr. Leslie Stephen, it seems, sees this clearly enough. Once give morality its spiritual and supernatural meaning, and there is, he holds, 'some underlying logical necessity which binds [a belief in hell] indissolubly with the primary articles of the faith.' Such a system of retribution, he adds, is 'created spontaneously' by the 'conscience. Heaven and hell are corollaries that rise and fall together.... Whatever the meaning of αιωνιος, the fearful emotion which is symbolised, is eternal or independent of time, by the same right as the ecstatic emotion.' He sees this clearly enough; but the strange thing is that he does not see the converse. He sees that the Christian conception of morality necessitates the affirmation of hell. He does not see that the denial of hell is the denial of Christian morality, and that in calling the former a dream, as he does, he does not call the latter a dream likewise.

We can close our eyes to none of these perplexities. The only way to resist their power is not to ignore them, but to realise to the full their magnitude, and to see how, if we let them take away from us anything, they will in another moment take everything; to see that we must either set our foot upon their necks, or that they will set their feet on ours; to see that we can look them down, but that we can never look them through; to see that we can make them impotent if we will, but that if they are not impotent they will be omnipotent.

But the strongest example of this is yet to come: and this is not any special belief either as to religion or morals, but a belief underlying both of these, and without which neither of them were possible. It is a belief which from one point of view we have already touched upon—the belief in the freedom of the will. But we have as yet only considered it in relation to physical science. What we have now to do is to consider it in relation to itself.

What, then, let us ask, is the nature of the belief? To a certain extent the answer is very easy. When we speak and think of free-will ordinarily, we know quite well what we mean by it; and we one and all of us mean exactly the same thing. It is true that when professors speak upon this question, they make countless efforts to distinguish between the meaning which they attach to the belief, and the meaning which the world attaches to it. And it is possible that in their studies or their lecture-rooms they may contrive for the time being to distort or to confuse for themselves the common view of the matter. But let the professor once forget his theories, and be forced to buffet against his life's importunate and stern realities: let him quarrel with his housekeeper because she has mislaid his spectacles, or his night-cap, or, preoccupied with her bible, has not mixed his gruel properly; and his conception of free-will will revert in an instant to the universal type, and the good woman will discern only too plainly that her master's convictions as to it are precisely the same things as her own. Everywhere, indeed, in all the life that surrounds us—in the social and moral judgments on which the fabric of society has reared itself, in the personal judgments on which so much depends in friendship and antipathies—everywhere, in conduct, in emotion, in art, in language, and in law, we see man's common belief in will written, broad, and plain, and clear. There is, perhaps, no belief to which, for practical purposes, he attaches so important and so plain a meaning.

Such is free-will when looked at from a distance. But let us look at it more closely, and see what happens then. The result is strange. Like a path seen at dusk across a moorland, plain and visible from a distance, but fading gradually from us the more near we draw to it, so does the belief in free-will fade before the near inspection of reason. It at first grows hazy; at last it becomes indistinguishable. At first we begin to be uncertain of what we mean by it; at last we find ourselves certain that so far as we trust to reason, we cannot possibly have any meaning at all. Examined in this way, every act of our lives—all our choices and refusals, seem nothing but the necessary outcome of things that have gone before. It is true that between some actions the choice hangs at times so evenly, that our will may seem the one thing that at last turns the balance. But let us analyse the matter a little more carefully, and we shall see that there are a thousand microscopic motives, too small for us to be entirely conscious of, which, according to how they settle on us, will really decide the question. Nor shall we see only that this is so. Let us go a little further, and reason will tell us that it must be so. Were this not the case, there would have been an escape left for us. Though admitting that what controlled our actions could be nothing but the strongest motive, it might yet be contended that the will could intensify any motive it chose, and that thus motives really were only tools in its hands. But this does but postpone the difficulty, not solve it. What is this free-will when it comes to use its tools? It is a something, we shall find, that our minds cannot give harbour to. It is a thing contrary to every analogy of nature. It is a thing which is forever causing, but which is in itself uncaused.

To escape from this difficulty is altogether hopeless. Age after age has tried to do so, but tried in vain. There have been always metaphysical experts ready to engage to make free-will a something intellectually conceivable. But they all either leave the question where they found it, or else they only seem to explain it, by denying covertly the fact that really wants explaining.

Such is free-will when examined by the natural reason—a thing that melts away inevitably first to haze, and then to utter nothingness. And for a time we feel convinced that it really is nothing. Let us, however, again retire from it to the common distance, and the phantom we thought exorcised is again back in an instant. There is the sphinx once more, distinct and clear as ever, holding in its hand the scales of good and evil, and demanding a curse or a blessing for every human action. We are once more certain—more certain of this than anything—that we are, as we always thought we were, free agents, free to choose, and free to refuse; and that in virtue of this freedom, and in virtue of this alone, we are responsible for what we do and are.

Let us consider this point well. Let us consider first how free-will is a moral necessity; next how it is an intellectual impossibility; and lastly how, though it be impossible, we yet, in defiance of intellect, continue, as moral beings, to believe in it. Let us but once realise that we do this, that all mankind universally do this and have done—and the difficulties offered us by theism will no longer stagger us. We shall be prepared for them, prepared not to drive them away, but to endure their presence.261 If in spite of my reason I can believe that my will is free, in spite of my reason I can believe that God is good. The latter belief is not nearly so hard as the former. The greatest stumbling-block in the moral world lies in the threshold by which to enter it.

Such then are the moral difficulties, properly so called, that beset theism; but there are certain others of a vaguer nature, that we must glance at likewise. It is somewhat hard to know how to classify these; but it will be correct enough to say that whereas those we have just dealt with appeal to the moral intellect, the ones we are to deal with now appeal to the moral imagination. The facts that these depend on, and which are practically new discoveries for the modern world, are the insignificance of the earth, when compared with the universe, of which it is visibly and demonstrably an integral but insignificant fragment; the enormous period of his existence for which man has had no religious history, and has been, so far as we can tell, not a religious being at all; and the vast majority of the race that are still stagnant and semi-barbarous. Is it possible, we ask, that a God, with so many stars to attend to, should busy himself with this paltry earth, and make it the scene of events more stupendous than the courses of countless systems? Is it possible that of the swarms, vicious and aimless, that breed upon it, each individual—Bushman,262 Chinaman, or Negro—is a precious immortal being, with a birthright in infinity and eternity? The effect of these considerations is sometimes overwhelming. Astronomy oppresses us with the gulfs of space; geology with the gulfs of time; history and travel with a babel of vain existence. And here as in the former case, our perplexities cannot be explained away. We can only meet them by seeing that if they have any power at all, they are all-powerful, and that they will not destroy religion only, but the entire moral conception of man also. Religious belief, and moral belief likewise, involve both of them some vast mystery; and reason can do nothing but focalise, not solve it.

All, then, that I am trying to make evident is this—and this must be sufficient for us—not that theism, with its attendant doctrines, presents us with no difficulties, necessitates no baffling contradictions in terms, and confronts us with no terrible and piteous spectacles, but that all this is not peculiar to theism. It is not the price we pay for rising from morality to religion. It is the price we pay for rising from the natural to the supernatural. Once double the sum of things by adding this second world to it, and it swells to such a size that our reason can no longer encircle it. We are torn this way and that by convictions, each of which is equally necessary, but each of which excludes the others. When we try to 263grasp them all at once, our mind is like a man tied to wild horses; or like Phaeton in the Sun's chariot, bewildered and powerless over the intractable and the terrible team. We can only recover our strength by a full confession of our weakness. We can only lay hold on the beliefs that we see to be needful, by asking faith to join hands with reason. If we refuse to do this, there is but one alternative. Without faith we can perhaps explain things if we will; but we must first make them not worth explaining. We can only think them out entirely by regarding them as something not worth thinking out at all.

Is Life Worth Living? By William Hurrell Mallock

CHAPTER XI.

THE HUMAN RACE AND REVELATION.

'The scandal of the pious Christian, and the fallacious triumph of the infidel, should cease as soon as they recollect not only by whom, but likewise to whom, the Divine Revelation was given.'—Gibbon.37

And now let us suppose ourselves convinced, at least for the sake of argument, that man will always believe in himself as a moral being, and that he will, under no compulsion, let this belief go. Granting this, from what we have just seen, thus much will be plain to us, that theism, should it ever tend to reassert itself, can have no check to fear at the hands of positive thought. Let us, therefore, suppose further, that such a revival of faith is imminent, and that the enlightened world, with its eyes wide open, is about to turn once again to religious desires and aims. This brings us face to face with the second question, that we have not as yet touched upon: will the religion thus turned to be a natural religion only, or is it possible that some exclusive dogmatism may be recognised as a supernatural re-statement of it?

Before going further with this question it will be well to say a few words as to the exact position it occupies. This, with regard to the needs of man, is somewhat different to the position of natural theism. That a natural theism is essential to man's moral being is a proposition that can be more or less rigidly demonstrated; but that a revelation is essential as a supplement to natural theism can be impressed upon us only in a much looser way. Indeed, many men who believe most firmly that without religion human life will be dead, rest their hopes for the future not on the revival and triumph of any one alleged revelation, but on the gradual evanescence of the special claims of all. Nor can we find any sharp and defined line of argument to convince them that they are wrong. The objections, however, to which this position is open are, I think, none the less cogent because they are somewhat general; and to all practical men, conversant with life and history, it must be plain that the necessity of doing God's will being granted, it is a most anxious and earnest question whether that will has not been in some special and articulate way revealed to us.

Take the mass of religious humanity, and giving it a natural creed, it will be found that instinctively and inevitably it asks for more. Such a creed by itself has excited more longings than it has satisfied, and raised more perplexities than it has set at rest. It is true that it has supplied men with a sufficient analysis of the worth they attach to life, and of the momentous issues attendant on the way in which they live it. But when they come practically to choose their way, they find that such religion is of little help to them. It never puts out a hand to lift or lead them. It is an alluring voice, heard far off through a fog, and calling to them, 'Follow me!' but it leaves them in the fog to pick their own way out towards it, over rocks and streams and pitfalls, which they can but half distinguish, and amongst which they may be either killed or crippled, and are almost certain to grow bewildered. And even should there be a small minority, who feel that this is not true of themselves, they can hardly help feeling that it is true of the world in general. A purely natural theism, with no organs of human speech, and with no machinery for making its spirit articulate, never has ruled men, and, so far as we can see, never possibly can rule them. The choices which our life consists of are definite things. The rule which is to guide our choices must be something definite also. And here it is that natural theism fails. It may supply us with the major premiss, but it is vague and uncertain about the minor. It can tell us with sufficient emphasis that all vice is to be avoided; it is continually at a loss to tell us whether this thing or whether that thing is vicious. Indeed, this practical insufficiency of natural theism is borne witness to by the very existence of all alleged revelations. For, if none of these be really the special word of God, a belief in them is all the more a sign of a general need in man. If none of them represent the actual attainment of help, they all of them embody the passionate and persistent cry for it.

We shall understand this more clearly if we consider one of the first characteristics that a revelation necessarily claims, and the results that are at this moment, in a certain prominent case, attending on a denial of it. The characteristic I speak of is an absolute infallibility. Any supernatural religion that renounces its claim to this, it is clear can profess to be a semi-revelation only. It is a hybrid thing, partly natural and partly supernatural, and it thus practically has all the qualities of a religion that is wholly natural. In so far as it professes to be revealed, it of course professes to be infallible; but if the revealed part be in the first place hard to distinguish, and in the second place hard to understand—if it may mean many things, and many of those things contradictory—it might just as well have been never made at all. To make it in any sense an infallible revelation, or in other words a revelation at all, to us, we need a power to interpret the testament that shall have equal authority with that testament itself.

Simple as this truth seems, mankind have been a long time in learning it. Indeed, it is only in the present day that its practical meaning has come generally to be recognised. But now at this moment upon all sides of us, history is teaching it to us by an example, so clearly that we can no longer mistake it.

That example is Protestant Christianity, and the condition to which, after three centuries, it is now visibly bringing itself. It is at last beginning to exhibit to us the true result of the denial of infallibility to a religion that professes to be supernatural. We are at last beginning to see in it neither the purifier of a corrupted revelation, nor the corrupter of a pure revelation, but the practical denier of all revelation whatsoever. It is fast evaporating into a mere natural theism, and is thus showing us what, as a governing power, natural theism is. Let us look at England, Europe, and America, and consider the condition of the entire Protestant world. Religion, it is true, we shall still find in it; but it is religion from which not only the supernatural element is disappearing, but in which the natural element is fast becoming nebulous. It is indeed growing, as Mr. Leslie Stephen says it is, into a religion of dreams. All its doctrines are growing vague as dreams, and like dreams their outlines are for ever changing. Mr. Stephen has pitched on a very happy 269illustration of this. A distinguished clergyman of the English Church, he reminds us, has preached and published a set of sermons,38 in which he denies emphatically any belief in eternal punishment, although admitting at the same time that the opinion of the Christian world is against him. These sermons gave rise to a discussion in one of the leading monthly reviews, to which Protestant divines of all shades of opinion contributed their various arguments. 'It is barely possible,' says Mr. Stephen, 'with the best intentions, to take such a discussion seriously. Boswell tells us how a lady interrogated Dr. Johnson as to the nature of the spiritual body. She seemed desirous, he adds, of "knowing more; but he left the subject in obscurity." We smile at Boswell's evident impression that Johnson could, if he had chosen, have dispelled the darkness. When we find a number of educated gentlemen seriously enquiring as to the conditions of existence in the next world, we feel that they are sharing Boswell's naïveté without his excuse. What can any human being outside a pulpit say upon such a subject which does not amount to a confession of his own ignorance, coupled, it may be, with more or less suggestion of shadowy hopes and fears? Have the secrets of the prison-house really been revealed to Canon Farrar or Mr. Beresford Hope?... When 270men search into the unknowable, they naturally arrive at very different results.' And Mr. Stephen argues with perfect justice that if we are to judge Christianity from such discussions as these, its doctrines of a future life are all visibly receding into a vague 'dreamland;' and we shall be quite ready to admit, as he says, in words I have already quoted, 'that the impertinent young curate who tells [him he] will be burnt everlastingly for not sharing such superstitions, is just as ignorant as [Mr. Stephen himself], and that [Mr. Stephen] knows as much as [his] dog.'

The critic, in the foregoing passages, draws his conclusion from the condition of but one Protestant doctrine. But he might draw the same conclusion from all; for the condition of all of them is the same. The divinity of Christ, the nature of his atonement, the constitution of the Trinity, the efficacy of the sacraments, the inspiration of the Bible—there is not one of these points on which the doctrines, once so fiercely fought for, are not now, among the Protestants, getting as vague and varying, as weak and as compliant to the caprice of each individual thinker, as the doctrine of eternal punishment. And Mr.

Stephen and his school exaggerate nothing in the way in which they represent the spectacle. Protestantism, in fact, is at last becoming explicitly what it always was implicitly, not a supernatural religion which fulfils the natural, but a natural religion which denies the supernatural.

And what, as a natural religion, is its working power in the world? Much of its earlier influence doubtless still survives; but that is a survival only of what is passing, and we must not judge it by that. We must judge it by what it is growing into, not by what it is growing out of. And judged in this way, its practical power—its moral, its teaching, its guiding power—is fast growing as weak and as uncertain as its theology. As long as its traditional moral system is in accordance with what men, on other grounds, approve of, it may serve to express the general tendency impressively, and to invest it with the sanction of many reverend associations. But let the general tendency once begin to conflict with it, and its inherent weakness in an instant becomes apparent. We may see this by considering the moral character of Christ, and the sort of weight that is claimed for His example. This example, so the Christian world teaches, is faultless and infallible; and as long as we believe this, the example has supreme authority. But apply to this the true Protestant method, and the authority soon shows signs of wavering. Let us once deny that Christ was more than a faultless man, and we lose by that denial our authority for asserting that he was as much as a faultless man. Even should it so happen that we do approve entirely of his conduct, it is we who are approving of him, not he who is approving of us. The old position is reversed: we become the patrons of our most worthy Judge eternal; and the moral infallibility is transferred from him to ourselves. In other words, the practical Protestant formula can be nothing more than this. The Protestant teacher says to us, 'Such a way of life is the best, take my word for it: and if you want an example, go to that excellent Son of David, who, take my word for it, was the very best of men.' But even in this case the question arises, how shall the Protestants interpret the character that they praise? And to this they can never give any satisfactory answer. What really happens with them is inevitable and obvious. The character is simply for them a symbol of what each happens to think most admirable; and the identity in all cases of its historical details does not produce an identity as of a single portrait, but an identity as of one frame applied to many. Mr. Matthew Arnold, for instance, sees in Jesus one sort of man, Father Newman another, Charles Kingsley another, and M. Renan another; and the Imitatio Christi, as understood by these, will be found in each case to mean a very different thing. The difference between these men, however, will seem almost unanimity, if we compare them with others who, so far as logic and authority go, have just as good a claim on our attention. There is hardly any conceivable aberration of moral licence that has not, in some quarter or other, embodied itself into a rule of life, and claimed to be the proper outcome of Protestant Christianity. Nor is this true only of the wilder and more eccentric sects. It is true of graver and more weighty thinkers also;

so much so, that a theological school in Germany has maintained boldly 'that fornication is blameless, and that it is not interdicted by the precepts of the Gospel.'39

The matter, however, does not end thus. The men I have just mentioned agree, all of them, that Christ's moral example was perfect; and their only disagreement has been as to what that example was. But the Protestant logic will by no means leave us here. That alleged perfection, if we ourselves are to be the judges of it, is sure, by-and-by, to exhibit to us traces of imperfection. And this is exactly the thing that has already begun to happen. A generation ago one of the highest-minded and most logical of our English Protestants, Professor Francis Newman, declared that in Christ's character there were certain moral deficiencies;40 and the last blow to the moral authority of Protestantism was struck by one of its own household. It is true that Professor Newman's censures were small and were not irreverent. But if these could come from a man of his intense piety, what will and what do come from other quarters may be readily conjectured. Indeed, the fact is daily growing more and more evident, that for the world that still calls itself Protestant, the autocracy of Christ's moral example is gone; and its nominal retention of power only makes its real loss of it the more visible. It merely reflects and focalises the uncertainty that men are again feeling—the uncertainty and the sad bewilderment. The words and the countenance, once so sure and steadfast, now change, as we look at, and listen to them, into new accents and aspects; and the more earnestly we gaze and listen, the less can we distinguish clearly what we hear or see. 'What shall we do to be saved?' men are again crying. And the lips that were once oracular now merely seem to murmur back confusedly, 'Alas! what shall you do?'

Such and so helpless, even now, is natural theism showing itself; and in the dim and momentous changes that are coming over things, in the vast flux of opinion that is preparing, in the earthquake that is rocking the moral ground under us, overturning and engulfing the former landmarks, and re-opening the graves of the buried lusts of paganism, it will show itself very soon more helpless still. Its feet are on the earth, only. The earth trembles, and it trembles: it is in the same case as we are. It stretches in vain its imploring hands to heaven. But the heaven takes no heed of it. No divine hand reaches down to it to uphold and guide it.

This must be the feeling, I believe, of most honest and practical men, with regard to natural religion, and its necessary practical inefficiency. Nor will the want it necessarily leaves of a moral rule be the only consideration that will force this conviction on them. The heart, as the phrase goes, will corroborate the evidence of the head. It will be felt, even more forcibly than it can be reasoned, that if there be indeed a God who loves and cares for men, he must surely, or almost surely, have spoken in some audible and certain way to them. At any rate I shall not be without many who agree with me, when I say that for the would-be religious world it is an anxious and earnest question whether any special and explicit revelation from God exist for us; and this being the case, it will be not lost time if we try to deal fairly and dispassionately with the question.

Before going further, however, let us call to mind two things. Let us remember first, that if we expect to find a revelation at all, it is morally certain that it must be a revelation already in existence. It is hardly possible, if we consider that all the supernatural claims that have been made hitherto are false, to expect that a new manifestation, altogether different in kind, is in store for the world in the future. Secondly, our enquiries being thus confined to religions that are already in existence, what we are practically concerned with is the truth of Christianity only. It is true that we have heard, on all sides, of the superiority of other religions to the Christian. But the men who hold such language, though they may affect to think that such religions are superior in certain moral points, yet never dream of claiming for them the miraculous and supernatural authority that they deny to Christianity. No man denies that Christ was born of a virgin, in order to make the same claim for Buddha: or denies the Christian Trinity in order to affirm the Brahminic. There is but one alleged revelation that, as a revelation, the progressive nations of the world are concerned with, or whose supernatural claims are still worthy of being examined by us: and that religion is the Christian. These claims, it is true, are being fast discredited; but still, as yet they have not been silenced wholly; and what I propose to ask now is, what chance is there of their power again reviving.

Now considering the way in which I have just spoken of Protestantism, it may seem to many that I have dismissed this question already. With the 'enlightened' English thinker such certainly will be the first impression. But there is one point that such thinkers all forget: Protestant Christianity is not the only form of it. They have still the form to deal with which is the oldest, the most legitimate, and the most coherent—the Church of Rome. They surely cannot forget the existence of this Church or her magnitude. To suppose this would be to attribute to them too insular, or rather too provincial, an ignorance. The cause, however, certainly is ignorance, and an ignorance which, though less surprising, is far deeper. In this country the popular conception of Rome has been so distorted by our familiarity with Protestantism, that the true conception of her is something quite strange to us. Our divines have exhibited her to us as though she were a lapsed Protestant sect, and they have attacked her for being false to doctrines that were never really hers. They have failed to see that the first and essential difference which separates her from them lies, primarily not in any special dogma, but in the authority on which all her dogmas rest. Protestants, basing their religion on the Bible solely, have conceived that Catholics of course profess to do so likewise; and have covered them with invective for being traitors to their supposed profession. But the Church's primary doctrine is her own perpetual infallibility. She is inspired, she declares, by the same Spirit that inspired the Bible; and her voice is, equally with the Bible, the voice of God. This theory, however, upon which really her whole fabric rests, popular

Protestantism either ignores altogether, or treats it as if it were a modern superstition, which, so far from being essential to the Church's system, is, on the contrary, inconsistent with it. Looked at in this way, Rome to the Protestant's mind has seemed naturally to be a mass of superstitions and dishonesties; and it is this view of her that, strangely enough, our modern advanced thinkers have accepted without question. Though they have trusted the Protestants in nothing else, they have trusted them here. They have taken the Protestants' word for it, that Protestantism is more reasonable than Romanism; and they think, therefore, that if they have destroyed the former, à fortiori have they destroyed the latter.41

No conception of the matter, however, could be more false than this. To whatever criticism the Catholic position may be open, it is certainly not thus included in Protestantism, nor is it reached through it. Let us try and consider the matter a little more truly. Let us grant all that hostile criticism can say against Protestantism as a supernatural religion: in other words, let us set it aside altogether. Let us suppose nothing, to start with, in the world but a natural moral sense, and a simple natural theism; and let us then see the relation of the Church of Rome to that. Approached in this way, the religious world will appear to us as a body of natural theists, all agreeing that they must do God's will, but differing widely amongst themselves as to what His will and His nature are. Their moral and religious views will be equally vague and dreamlike—more dreamlike even than those of the Protestant world at present. Their theories as to the future will be but 'shadowy hopes and fears.' Their practice, in the present, will vary from asceticism to the widest license. And yet, in spite of all this confusion and difference, there will be amongst them a vague tendency to unanimity. Each man will be dreaming his own spiritual dream, and the dreams of all will be different. All their dreams, it will be plain, cannot represent reality; and yet the belief will be common to all that some common reality is represented by them. Men, therefore, will begin to compare their dreams together, and try to draw out of them the common element, so that the dream may come slowly to be the same for all; that, if it grows, it may grow by some recognizable laws; that it may, in other words, lose its character of a dream, and assume that of a reality. We suppose, therefore, that our natural theists form themselves into a kind of parliament, in which they may compare, adjust, and give shape to the ideas that were before so wavering, and which shall contain some machinery for formulating such agreements as may be come to. The common religious sense of the world is thus organized, and its conclusions registered. We have no longer the wavering dreams of men; we have instead of them the constant vision of man.

Now in such a universal parliament we see what the Church of Rome essentially is, viewed from her natural side. She is ideally, if not actually, the parliament of the believing world. Her doctrines, as she one by one unfolds them, emerge upon us like petals from a half-closed bud. They are not added arbitrarily from without; they are developed from within. They are the flowers contained from the first in the bud of our moral consciousness. When she formulates in these days something that has not been formulated before, she is no more enunciating a new truth than was Newton when he enunciated the theory of gravitation. Whatever truths, hitherto hidden, she may in the course of time grow conscious of, she holds that these were always implied in her teaching, though before she did not know it; just as gravitation was implied in many ascertained facts that men knew well enough long before they knew that it was implied in them. Thus far, then, the Church of Rome essentially is the spiritual sense of humanity, speaking to men through its proper and only possible organ. Its intricate machinery, such as its systems of representation, its methods of voting, the appointment of its speaker, and the legal formalities required in the recording of its decrees, are things accidental only; or if they are necessary, they are necessary only in a secondary way.

But the picture of the Church thus far is only half drawn. She is all this, but she is something more than this. She is not only the parliament of spiritual man, but she is such a parliament guided by the Spirit of God. The work of that Spirit may be secret, and to the natural eyes untraceable, as the work of the human will is in the human brain. But none the less it is there.

Totam infusa per artus
Mens agitat molem, et magno se corpore miscet.
The analogy of the human brain is here of great help to us. The human brain is an arrangement of material particles which can become connected with consciousness only in virtue of such a special arrangement. The Church is theoretically an arrangement of individuals which can become connected with the Spirit of God only in virtue of an arrangement equally special.

If this be a true picture of the Catholic Church, and the place which the only revelation we are concerned with ideally holds in the world, there can be no à priori difficulty in the passage from a natural religion to such a supernatural one. The difficulties begin when we compare the ideal picture with the actual facts; and it is true, when we do this, that they at once confront us with a strength that seems altogether disheartening. These difficulties are of two distinct kinds; some, as in the case of natural theism, are moral; others are historical. We will deal with the former first, beginning with that which is at once the profoundest and the most obvious.

The Church, as has been said already, is ideally the parliament of the whole believing world; but we find, as a matter of fact, that she is the parliament of a small part only. Now what shall we say to this? If God would have all men do His will, why should He place the knowledge of it within reach of such a small minority of them? And to this question we can give no answer. It is a mystery, and we must acknowledge frankly that it is one. But there is this to say yet—that it is not a new mystery. We already suppose ourselves to have accepted it in a simpler form: in the form of the presence of evil, and the partial prevalence of good. By acknowledging the claim of the special revelation in question, we are not adding to the complexity of that old world-problem. I am aware, however, that many think just the reverse of this. I will therefore dwell upon the subject for a few moments longer. To many who can accept the difficulty of the partial presence of good, the difficulty seems wantonly aggravated by the claims of a special revelation. These claims seem to them to do two things. In the first place, they are thought to make the presence of good even more partial than it otherwise would be; and secondly—which is a still greater stumbling-block—to oblige us to condemn as evil much that would else seem good of the purest kind. There are many men, as we must all know, without the Church, who are doing their best to fight their way to God; and orthodoxy is supposed to pass a cruel condemnation on these, because they have not assented to some obscure theory, their rejection or ignorance of which has plainly stained neither their lives nor hearts. And of orthodoxy under certain forms this is no doubt true; but it is not true of the orthodoxy of Catholicism. There is no point, probably, connected with this question, about which the general world is so misinformed and ignorant, as the sober but boundless charity of what it calls the anathematising Church. So little indeed is this charity understood generally, that to assert it seems a startling paradox. Most paradoxes are doubtless in reality the lies they at first sight seem to be; but not so this one. It is the simple statement of a fact. Never was there a religious body, except the Roman, that laid the intense stress she does on all her dogmatic teachings, and had yet the justice that comes of sympathy for those that cannot receive them. She condemns no goodness, she condemns even no earnest worship, though it be outside her pale. On the contrary, she declares explicitly that a knowledge of 'the one true God, our Creator and Lord,' may be attained to by the 'natural light of human reason,' meaning by 'reason' faith unenlightened by revelation; and she declares those to be anathema who deny this. The holy and humble men of heart who do not know her, or who in good faith reject her, she commits with confidence to God's uncovenanted mercies; and these she knows are infinite; but, except as revealed to her, she can of necessity say nothing distinct about them. It is admitted by the world at large, that of her supposed bigotry she has no bitterer or more extreme exponents than the Jesuits; and this is what a Jesuit theologian says upon this matter: 'A heretic, so long as he believes his sect to be more or equally deserving of belief, has no obligation to believe the Church ... [and] when men who have been brought up in heresy, are persuaded from boyhood that we impugn and attack the word of God, that we are idolaters, pestilent deceivers, and are therefore to be shunned as pestilence, they cannot, while this persuasion lasts, with a safe conscience hear us.'[42] Thus for those without her the Church has one condemnation only. Her anathemas are on none but those who reject her with their eyes open, by tampering with a conviction that she really is the truth. These are condemned, not for not seeing that the teacher is true, but because having really seen this, they continue to close their eyes to it. They will not obey when they know they ought to obey. And thus the moral offence of a Catholic in denying some recondite doctrine, does not lie merely, and need not lie at all, in the immediate bad effects that such a denial would necessitate; but in the disobedience, the self-will, and the rebellion that must in such a case be both a cause and a result of it.

In the light of these considerations, though the old perplexity of evil will still confront us, it will be seen that the claims of Catholic orthodoxy do nothing at all to add to it. If orthodoxy, however, admit so much good without itself, we may perhaps be inclined to ask what special good it claims within itself, and what possible motives can exist for either understanding or teaching it. But we might ask with exactly equal force, what is the good of true physical science, and why should we try to impress on the world its teachings? Such a question, we can at once see, is absurd. Because a large number of men know nothing of physical science, and are apparently not the worse for their ignorance, we do not for that reason think physical science worthless. We believe, on the whole, that a knowledge of the laws of matter, including those of our organisms and their environments, will steadily tend to better our lives, in so far as they are material. It will tend, for instance, to a better preservation of our health. But we do not for this reason deny that many individuals may preserve their health who are but very partially acquainted with the laws of it. Nor do we deny the value of a thorough study of astronomy and meteorology because a certain practical knowledge of the weather and of navigation may be attained without it. On the contrary, we hold that the fullest knowledge we can acquire on such matters it is our duty to acquire, and not acquire only, but as far as possible promulgate. It is true that the mass of men may never master such knowledge thoroughly; but what they do master of it we feel convinced should be the truth, and even what they do not, will, we feel convinced, be some indirect profit to them. And the case of spiritual science is entirely analogous to the case of natural science. A man to whom the truth is open is not excused from finding it because he knows it is not so open to all. A heretic who denies the dogmas of the Church has his counterpart in the quack who denies the verified conclusions of science. The moral condemnation that is given to the one is illustrated by the intellectual condemnation that is given to the other.

If we will think this over carefully, we shall get a clearer view of the moral value claimed for itself by orthodoxy. Some of its doctrines, the great and picturable parts of them, that appeal to all, and that in some degree can be taken in by all, it declares doubtless to be saving, in their own nature. But for the mass of men the case is quite different with the facts underlying these. That we eat Christ's body in the Eucharist is a belief that, in a practical way, can be understood perfectly by anyone; but the philosophy that is involved in this belief would be to most men the merest gibberish. Yet it is no more unimportant that those who do understand this philosophy, should do so truly and transmit it faithfully, than it is unimportant that a physician should understand the action of alcohol, because anyone independent of such knowledge can tell that so many glasses of wine will have such and such an effect on him. Theology is to the spiritual body what anatomy and medicine are to the natural body. The parts they each play in our lives are analogous, and in their respective worlds their raison d'être is the same. What then can be shallower than the rhetoric of such thinkers as Mr. Carlyle, in which natural religion and orthodoxy are held up to us as contrasts and as opposites, the former being praised as simple and going straight to the heart, and the latter described and declaimed against as the very reverse of this? 'On the one hand,' it is said, 'see the soul going straight to its God, feeling His love, and content that others should feel it. On the other hand, see this pure and free communion, distracted and interrupted by a thousand tortuous reasonings as to the exact nature of it. What can obscure intellectual propositions,' it is asked, 'have to do with a religion of the heart? And do not they check the latter by being thus bound up with it?' But what really can be more misleading than this? Natural religion is doubtless simpler in one sense than revealed religion; but it is only simple because it has no authoritative science of itself. It is simple for the same reason that a boy's account of having given himself a headache is simpler than a physician's would be. The boy says merely, 'I ate ten tarts, and drank three bottles of ginger-beer.' The physician, were he to explain the catastrophe, would describe a number of far more complex processes. The boy's account would be of course the simplest, and would certainly go more home to the general heart of boyhood; but it would not for that reason be the correctest or the most important. And just like this will be the case of the divine communion, which the simple saint may feel, and the subtle theologian analyse.

But it will be well to observe, further, that the simplicity of a religion can of itself be no test of the probable truth of it. And in the case of natural religion, what is called simplicity is in general nothing more than vagueness. If simplicity used in this way be a term of praise, we might praise a landscape as simple because it was half-drowned in mist. As a matter of fact, however, the religion of the Catholic Church, putting out of the question its theology, is a thing far simpler than the outside world supposes; nor is there a doctrine in it without a direct moral meaning for us, and not tending to have a direct effect on the character.

But the outside world misjudges of all this for various reasons. In the first place, it can reach it as a rule through explanations only; and the explanation or the account of anything is always far more intricate than the apprehension of the thing itself. Take, for instance, the practice of the invocation of saints. This seems to many to complicate the whole relation of the soul to God, to be introducing a number of new and unnecessary go-betweens, and to make us, as it were, communicate with God through a dragoman. But the case really is very different. Of course it may be contended that intercessory prayer, or that prayer of any kind, is an absurdity; but for those who do not think this, there can be nothing to object to in the invocation of saints. It is admitted by such men that we are not wrong in asking the living to pray for us. Surely, therefore, it is not wrong to make a like request of the dead. In the same way, to those who believe in purgatory, to pray for the dead is as natural and as rational as to pray for the living. Next, as to this doctrine of purgatory itself—which has so long been a stumbling-block to the whole Protestant world—time goes on, and the view men take of it is changing. It is becoming fast recognized on all sides that it is the only doctrine that can bring a belief in future rewards and punishments into anything like accordance with our notions of what is just or reasonable. So far from its being a superfluous superstition, it is seen to be just what is demanded at once by reason and morality; and a belief in it to be not an intellectual assent only, but a partial harmonising of the whole moral ideal. And the whole Catholic religion, if we only distinguish and apprehend it rightly, will present itself to us in the same light.

But there are other reasons besides those just described, by which outsiders are hindered from arriving at such a right view of the matter. Not only does the intricacy of Catholicism described, blind them to the simplicity of Catholicism experienced, but they confuse with the points of faith, not only the scientific accounts the theologians give of them, but mere rules of discipline, and pious opinions also. It is supposed popularly, for instance, to be of Catholic faith that celibacy is essential to the priesthood. This as a fact, however, is no more a part of the Catholic faith than the celibacy of a college fellow is a part of the Thirty-nine Articles, or than the skill of an English naval officer depends on his not having his wife with him on shipboard. Nor again, to take another popular instance, is the headship of the Catholic Church connected essentially with Rome, any more than the English Parliament is essentially connected with Westminster.

The difficulty of distinguishing things that are of faith, from mere pious opinions, is a more subtle one. From the confusion caused by it, the Church seems pledged to all sorts of grotesque stories of saints, and accounts of the place and aspect of heaven, of hell and purgatory, and to be logically bound to stand and fall by these. Thus Sir James Stephen happened once in the course of his reading to light on an opinion of Bellarmine's, and certain arguments by which he supported it, as to the place of purgatory. It is quite true that to us Bellarmine's opinion seems sufficiently ludicrous; and Sir James Stephen argued that the Roman Church is ludicrous in just the same degree. But if he had studied the matter a little deeper, he would soon have dropped his argument. He would have seen that he was attacking, not the doctrine of the Church, but simply an opinion, not indeed condemned by her, but held avowedly without her sanction. Had he studied Bellarmine to a little more purpose, he would have seen that that writer expressly states it to be 'a question where purgatory is, but that the Church has defined nothing on this point.' He would also have learned from the same source that it is no article of Catholic faith, though it was of Bellarmine's opinion, that there is in purgatory any material fire; and that, 'as to the intensity of the pains of purgatory, though all admit that they are greater than anything that we suffer in this life, still it is doubtful how this is to be explained and understood.' He would have learned too that, according to Bonaventura, 'the sufferings of purgatory are only severer than those of this life, inasmuch as the greatest suffering in purgatory is more severe than the greatest suffering endured in this life; though there may be a degree of punishment in purgatory less intense than what may sometimes be undergone in this world.' And finally he would have learned—what in this connection would have been well worth his attention—that the duration of pains in purgatory is according to Bellarmine, 'so completely uncertain, that it is rash to pretend to determine anything about it.'

Here is one instance, that will be as good as many, of the way in which the private opinions of individual Catholics, or the transitory opinions of particular epochs, are taken for the unalterable teachings of the Catholic Church herself; and it is no more logical to condemn the latter as false because the former are, than it would be to say that all modern geography is false because geographers may still entertain false opinions about regions as to which they do not profess certainty. Mediæval doctors thought that purgatory might be the middle of the earth. Modern geographers have thought that there might be an open sea at the North Pole. But that wrong conjectures have been hazarded in both cases, can prove in neither that there have been no true discoveries. The Church, it is undeniable, has for a long time lived and moved amongst countless false opinions; and to the external eye they have naturally seemed a part of her. But science moves on, and it is shown that she can cast them off. She has cast off some already; soon doubtless she will cast off others; not in any petulant anger, but with a composed determined gentleness, as some new light gravely dawns upon her.

Granting all this, however, there remains a yet subtler characteristic of the Church, which goes to make her a rock of offence to many; and that is, the temper and the intellectual tone which she seems to develop in her members. But here, again, we must call to our aid considerations similar to those we have just been dwelling on. We must remember that the particular tone and temper that offends us is not necessarily Catholicism. The temper of the Catholic world may change, and, as a matter of fact, does change. It is not the same, indeed, in any two countries, or in any two eras. And it may have a new and unsuspected future in store for it. It may absorb ideas that we should consider broader, bolder, and more rational than any it seems to possess at present. But if ever it does so, the Church, in the opinion of Catholics, will not be growing false to herself; she will only, in due time, be unfolding her own spirit more fully. Thus some people associate Catholic conceptions of extreme sanctity with a neglect of personal cleanliness; and imagine that a clean Catholic can, according to his own creed, never come very near perfection. But the Church has never given this view her sanction; she has never made it of faith that dirt is sacred; she has added no ninth beatitude in favour of an unchanged shirt. Many of the greatest saints were doubtless dirty; but they were dirty not because of the Church they belonged to, but because of the age they lived in. Such an expression of sanctity for themselves, it is probable, will be loathed by the saints of the future; yet they may none the less reverence, for all that, the saints who so expressed it in the past. This is but a single instance; but it may serve as a type of the wide circle of changes that the Church as a living organism, still full of vigour and power of self-adaptation, will be able to develop, as the world develops round her, and yet lose nothing of her supernatural sameness.

To sum up, then; if we would obtain a true view of the general character of Catholicism, we must begin by making a clean sweep of all the views that, as outsiders, we have been taught to entertain about her. We must, in the first place, learn to conceive of her as a living, spiritual body, as infallible and as authoritative now as she ever was, with her eyes undimmed and her strength not abated, continuing to grow still as she has continued to grow hitherto: and the growth of the new dogmas that she may from time to time enunciate, we must learn to see are, from her own stand-point, signs of life and not signs of corruption. And further, when we come to look into her more closely, we must separate carefully the diverse elements we find in her—her discipline, her pious opinions, her theology, and her religion.

Let honest enquirers do this to the best of their power, and their views will undergo an unlooked-for change. Other difficulties of a more circumstantial kind, it is true, still remain for them; and of these I shall speak presently. But putting these for the moment aside, and regarding the question under its widest aspects only—regarding it only in connection with the larger generalisations of science, and the primary postulates of man's spiritual existence—the theist will find in Catholicism no new difficulties. He will find in it the logical development of our natural moral sense, developed, indeed, and still developing, under a special and supernatural care—but essentially the same thing; with the same negations, the same assertions, the same positive truths, and the same impenetrable mysteries; and with nothing new added to them, but help, and certainty, and guidance.

Is Life Worth Living? By William Hurrell Mallock

CHAPTER XII.

UNIVERSAL HISTORY AND THE CLAIMS OF THE CHRISTIAN CHURCH.

Oh the little more, and how much it is,
And the little less, and what worlds away!—Robert Browning.

And now we come to the last objections left us, of those which modern thought has arrayed against the Christian Revelation; and these to many minds are the most conclusive and overwhelming of all—the objections raised against it by a critical study of history. Hitherto we have been considering the Church only with reference to our general sense of the fitness and the rational probability of things. We have now to consider her with reference to special facts. Her claims and her character, as she exists at present, may make perhaps appeal overpoweringly to us; but she cannot be judged only by these. For these are closely bound up with a long earthly history, which the Church herself has written in one way, binding herself to stand or fall by the truth of it; and this all the secular wisdom of the world seems to be re-writing in quite another. This subject is so vast and intricate that even to approach the details of it would require volumes, not a single chapter. But room in a chapter may be found for one thing, of prior importance to any mass of detail; and that is a simple statement of the principles—unknown to, or forgotten by external critics—by which all this mass of detail is to be interpreted.

Let us remember first, then, to take a general view of the matter, that history as cited in witness against the Christian Revelation, divides itself into two main branches. The one is a critical examination of Christianity, taken by itself—the authorship, and the authenticity of its sacred books, and the origin and growth of its doctrines. The other is a critical examination of Christianity as compared with other religions. And the result of both these lines of study is, to those brought up in the old faith, to the last degree startling, and in appearance at least altogether disastrous. Let us sum up briefly the general results of them; and first of these the historical.

We shall begin naturally with the Bible, as giving us the earliest historical point at which Christianity is assailable. What then has modern criticism accomplished on the Bible? The Biblical account of the creation it has shown to be, in its literal sense, an impossible fable. To passages thought mystical and prophetic it has assigned the homeliest, and often retrospective meanings. Everywhere at its touch what seemed supernatural has been humanized, and the divinity that hedged the records has rapidly abandoned them. And now looked at in the common daylight their whole aspect changes for us; and stories that we once accepted with a solemn reverence seem childish, ridiculous, grotesque, and not unfrequently barbarous. Or if we are hardly prepared to admit so much as this, this much at least has been established firmly—that the Bible, if it does not give the lie itself to the astonishing claims that have been made for it, contains nothing in itself, at any rate, that can of itself be sufficient to support them. This applies to the New Testament just as much as to the Old; and the consequences here are even more momentous. Weighed as mere human testimony, the value of the Gospels becomes doubtful or insignificant. For the miracles of Christ, and for his superhuman nature, they contain little evidence, that even tends to be satisfactory; and even his daily words and actions it seems probable may have been inaccurately reported, in some cases perhaps invented, and in others supplied by a deceiving memory. When we pass from the Gospels to the Epistles, a kindred sight presents itself. We discern in them the writings of men not inspired from above; but, with many disagreements amongst themselves, struggling upwards from below, influenced by a variety of existing views, and doubtful which of them to assimilate. We discern in them, as we do in other writers, the products of their age and of their circumstances. The materials out of which they formed their doctrines we can find in the lay world around them. And as we follow the Church's history farther, and examine the appearance and the growth of her great subsequent dogmas, we can trace all of them to a natural and a non-Christian origin. We can see, for instance, how in part, at least, men conceived the idea of the Trinity from the teachings of Greek Mysticism; and how the theory of the Atonement was shaped by the ideas of Roman Jurisprudence. Everywhere, in fact, in the holy building supposed to have come down from God, we detect fragments of older structures, confessedly of earthly workmanship.

But the matter does not end here. Historical science not only shows us Christianity, with its sacred history, in this new light; but it sets other religions by the side of it, and shows us that their course through the world has been strangely similar. They too have had their sacred books, and their incarnate Gods for prophets; they have had their priesthoods, their traditions, and their growing bodies of doctrine: there is nothing in Christianity that cannot find its counterpart, even to the most marked details, in the life of its founder. Two centuries, for instance, before the birth of Christ, Buddha is said to have been born without human father. Angels sang in heaven to announce his advent; an aged hermit blessed him in his mother's arms; a monarch was advised, though he refused, to destroy the child, who, it was predicted, should be a universal ruler. It is told how he was once lost, and was found again in a temple; and how his young wisdom astonished all the doctors. A woman in a crowd was rebuked by him for exclaiming, 'Blessed is the womb that bare thee.' His prophetic career began when he was about thirty years old; and one of the most solemn events of it is his temptation in solitude by the evil one. Everywhere, indeed, in other religions we are discovering things that we once thought peculiar to the Christian. And thus the fatal inference is being drawn on all sides, that they have all sprung from a common and an earthly root, and that one has no more certainty than another. And thus another blow is dealt to a faith that was already weakened. Not only, it is thought, can Christianity not prove itself in any supernatural sense to be sacred, but other religions prove that even in a natural sense it is not singular. It has not come down from heaven: it is not exceptional even in its attempt to rise to it.

Such are the broad conclusions which in these days seem to be forced upon us; and which knowledge, 302as it daily widens, would seem to be daily strengthening. But are these altogether so destructive as they seem? Let us enquire into this more closely. If we do this, it will be soon apparent that the so-called enlightened and critical modern judgment has been misled as to this point by an error I have already dwelt upon. It has considered Christianity solely as represented by Protestantism; or if it has glanced at Rome at all, it has ignorantly dismissed as weaknesses the doctrines which are the essence of her strength. Now, as far as Protestantism is concerned, the modern critical judgment is undoubtedly in the right. Not only, as I have pointed out already, has experience proved the practical incoherency of its superstructure, but criticism has washed away like sand every vestige of its supernatural foundation. If Christianity relies solely, in proof of its revealed message to us, on the external evidences as to its history and the source of its doctrines, it can never again hope to convince men. The supports of external evidence are quite inadequate to the weight that is put upon them. They might possibly serve as props; but they crush and crumble instantly, when they are used as pillars. And as pillars it is that Protestantism is compelled to use them. It will be quite sufficient, here, to confine our attention to the Bible, and the place which it occupies in the structure of the Protestant fabric. 'There—in that303 book,' says Protestantism, 'is the Word of God; there is my unerring guide; I listen to none but that. All special Churches have varied, and have therefore erred; but it is my first axiom that that book has never erred. On that book, and on that book only, do I rest myself; and out of its mouth shall you judge me.' And for a long time this language had much force in it; for the Protestant axiom was received by all parties. It is true, indeed, as we have seen already, that in the absence of an authoritative interpreter, an ambiguous testament would itself have little authority. But it took a long time for men to perceive this; and all admitted meanwhile that the testament was there, and it at any rate meant something. But now all this is changed. The great Protestant axiom is received by the world no longer. To many it seems not an axiom, but an absurdity; at best it appears but as a very doubtful fact: and if external proof is to be the thing that guides us, we shall need more proof to convince us that the Bible is the Word of God, than that Protestantism is the religion of the Bible.

We need not pursue the enquiry further, nor ask how Protestantism will fare at the hands of Comparative Mythology. The blow dealt by Biblical criticism is to all appearances mortal, and there is no need to look about for a second. But let us turn to Catholicism, and we shall see that the whole case is different. To its past history, to external evidence, and to the religions outside itself, Protestant Christianity bears one relation, and Roman Christianity quite another.

Protestantism offers itself to the world as a strange servant might, bringing with it a number of written testimonials. It asks us to examine them, and by them to judge of its merits. It expressly begs us not to trust to its own word. 'I cannot,' it says, 'rely upon my memory. It has failed me often; it may fail me again. But look at these testimonials in my favour, and judge me only by them.' And the world looks at them, examines them carefully; it at last sees that they look suspicious, and that they may, very possibly, be forgeries. It ask the Protestant Church to prove them genuine; and the Protestant Church cannot.

But the Catholic Church comes to us in an exactly opposite way. She too brings with her the very same testimonials; but she knows the uncertainty that obscures all remote evidences, and so at first she does not lay much stress upon them. First she asks us to make some acquaintance with herself; to look into her living eyes, to hear the words of her mouth, to watch her ways and works, and to feel her inner spirit; and then she says to us, 'Can you trust me? If you can, you must trust me all in all; for the very first thing I declare to you is, I have never lied. Can you trust me thus far? Then listen, and I will tell you my history. You have heard it told one way, I know; and that way often goes against me. My career, I admit it myself, has many suspicious circumstances. But none of them positively condemn me: all are capable of a guiltless interpretation. And when you know me, as I am, you will give me the benefit of every doubt.' It is thus that the Catholic Church presents the Bible to us. 'Believe the Bible, for my sake,' she says, 'not me for the Bible's.' And the book, as thus offered us, changes its whole character. We have not the formal testimonials of a stranger; we have instead the memoranda of a friend. We have now that presumption in their favour that in the former case was wanting altogether; and all that we ask of the records now is, not that they contain any inherent evidence of their truth, but that they contain no inherent evidence of their falsehood.

Farther, there is this point to remember. Catholic and Protestant alike declare the Bible to be inspired. But the Catholics can attach to inspiration a far wider, and less assailable meaning: for their Church claims for herself a perpetual living power, which can always concentrate the inspired element, be it never so diffused; whereas for the Protestants, unless that element be closely bound up with the letter, it at once becomes intangible and eludes them altogether. And thus, whilst the latter have committed themselves to definite statements, now proved untenable, as to what inspiration is, the Catholic Church, strangely enough, has never done anything of the kind. She has declared nothing on the subject that is to be held of faith. The whole question is still, within limits, an open one. As the Catholic Church, then, stands at present, it seems hard to say that, were we for other reasons inclined to trust her, she makes any claims, on behalf of her sacred books, which, in the face of impartial history, would prevent our doing so.

Let us now go farther, and consider those great Christian doctrines which, though it is claimed that they are all implied in the Bible, are confessedly not expressed in it, and were confessedly not consciously assented to by the Church, till long after the Christian Canon was closed. And here let us grant the modern critics their most hostile and extreme position. Let us grant that all the doctrines in question can be traced to external, and often to non-Christian sources. And what is the result on Romanism? Does this logically go any way whatever towards discrediting its claims? Let us consider the matter fairly, and we shall see that it has not even a tendency to do so. Here, as in the case of the Bible, the Church's doctrine of her infallibility meets all objections. For the real question here is, not in what storehouse of opinions the Church found her doctrines, but why she selected those she did, and why she rejected and condemned the rest. History and scientific criticism cannot answer this. History can show us only who baked the separate bricks; it cannot show us who made or designed the building. No one believes that the devil made the plans of Cologne Cathedral; but were we inclined to think he did, the story would be disproved in no way by our discovering from what quarries every stone had been taken. And the doctrines of the Church are but as the stones in a building, the letters of an alphabet, or the words of a language. Many are offered and few chosen. The supernatural action is to be detected in the choice. The whole history of the Church, in fact, as she herself tells it, may be described as a history of supernatural selection. It is quite possible that she may claim it to be more than that; but could she vindicate for herself but this one faculty of an infallible choice, she would vindicate to the full her claim to be under a superhuman guidance.

The Church may be conceived of as a living organism, for ever and on all sides putting forth feelers and tentacles, that seize, try, and seem to dally with all kinds of nutriment. A part of this she at length takes into herself. A large part she at length puts down again. Much that is thus rejected she seems for a long time on the point of choosing. But however slow may be the final decision in coming, however reluctant or hesitating it may seem to be, when it is once made, it is claimed for it that it is infallible. And this claim is one, as we shall see when we understand its nature, that no study of ecclesiastical history, no study of comparative mythology can invalidate now, or even promise to invalidate. There is nothing rash in saying this. The Church knows the difficulties that her past records present to us, especially that of the divine character of the Bible. But she knows too that this divinity is at present protected by its vagueness; nor is she likely to expose it more openly to its enemies, till some sure plan of defence has been devised for it. Rigid as were the opinions entertained as to Biblical inspiration, throughout the greater part of the Church's history, the Church has never formally assumed them as articles of faith. Had she done so, she might indeed have been convicted of error, for many of these opinions can be shown to be at variance with fact. But though she lived and breathed for so many centuries amongst them, though for ages none of her members perhaps ever doubted their truth, she has not laid them on succeeding ages: she has left them opinions still. A Catholic might well adduce this as an instance, not indeed of her supernatural selection, but of its counterpart, her supernatural rejection.

And now, to turn from the past to the future, her possible future conduct in this matter will give us a very vivid illustration of her whole past procedure. It may be that before the Church defines inspiration exactly (if she ever does so), she will wait till lay criticism has done all it can do. She may then consider what views of the Bible are historically tenable, and what not; and may faithfully shape her teaching by the learning of this world, though it may have been gathered together for the express purpose of overthrowing her. Atheistic scholars may be quoted in her councils; and supercilious and sceptical philologists, could they live another hundred years, might perhaps recognise their discoveries, even their words and phrases, embodied in an ecclesiastical definition. To the outer world such a definition would seem to be a mere natural production. But in the eyes of a Catholic it would be as truly supernatural, as truly the work of the Holy Spirit, as if it had come down ready-made out of heaven, with all the accompaniments of a rushing mighty wind, and of visible tongues of flame. Sanguine critics might expose the inmost history of the council in which the definition was made; they might show the whole conduct of it, from one side, to be but a meshwork of accident and of human motives; and they would ask triumphantly for any traces of the action of the divine spirit. But the Church, would be unabashed. She would answer in the words of Job, 'Behold I go forward, but He is not there; and backward, but I cannot perceive Him; but He knoweth the way that I take; when He hath tried me, I shall come forth as gold. Behold my witness is in heaven, and my champion is on high.'

And thus the doctrine of the Church's infallibility has a side that is just the opposite of that which is commonly thought to be its only one. It is supposed to have simply gendered bondage; not to have gendered liberty. But as a matter of fact it has done both; and if we view the matter fairly, we shall see that it has done the latter at least as completely as the former. The doctrine of infallibility is undoubtedly a rope that tethers those that hold it to certain real or supposed facts of the past; but it is a rope that is capable of indefinite lengthening. It is not a fetter only; it is a support also; and those who cling to it can venture fearlessly, as explorers, into currents of speculation that would sweep away altogether men who did but trust to their own powers of swimming. Nor does, as is often supposed, the centralizing of this infallibility in the person of one man present any difficulty from the Catholic point of view. It is said that the Pope might any day make a dogma of any absurdities that might happen to occur to him; and that the Catholic would be bound to accept these, however strongly his reason might repudiate them. And it is quite true that the Pope might do this any day, in the sense that there is no external power to prevent him. But he who has assented to the central doctrine of Catholicism knows that he never will. And it is precisely the obvious absence of any restraint from without that brings home to the Catholic his faith in the guiding power from within.

Such, then, and so compacted is the Church of Rome, as a visible and earthly body, with a past and future history. And with so singular a firmness and flexibility is her frame knit together, that none of her modern enemies can get any lasting hold on her, or dismember her or dislocate her limbs on the racks of their criticism.

But granting all this, what does this do for her? Does it do more than present her to us as the toughest and most fortunate religion, out of many co-ordinate and competing ones? Does it tend in any way to set her on a different platform from the others? And the answer to this is, that, so far as exact proof goes, we have nothing to expect or deal with in the matter, either one way or the other. The evidences at our disposal will impart a general tendency to our opinions, but no more than that. The general tendency here, however, is the very reverse of what it is vulgarly supposed to be. So far from the similarities to her in other religions telling against the special claims of the Catholic Church, they must really, with the candid theist, tell very strongly in her favour. For the theist, all theisms have a profound element of truth in them; and all alleged revelations will, in his eyes, be natural theisms, struggling to embody themselves in some authorised and authoritative form. The Catholic Church, as we have seen, is a human organism, capable of receiving the Divine Spirit; and this is what all other religious bodies, in so far as they have claimed authority for their teaching, have consciously or unconsciously attempted to be likewise; only the Catholic Church represents success, where the others represent failure: and thus these, from the Catholic stand-point, are abortive and incomplete Catholicisms. The Bethesda of human faith is world-wide and as old as time; only in one particular spot an angel has come down and troubled it; and the waters have been circling there, thenceforth, in a healing vortex. Such is the sort of claim that the Catholic Church makes for herself; and, if this be so, what she is, does not belie what she claims to be. Indeed, the more we compare her with the other religions, her rivals, the more, even where she most resembles them, shall we see in her a something that marks her off from them. The others are like vague and vain attempts at a forgotten tune; she is like the tune itself, which is recognised the instant it is heard, and which has been so near to us all the time, though so immeasurably far away from us. The Catholic Church is the only dogmatic religion that has seen what dogmatism really implies, and what will, in the long run, be demanded of it, and she contains in herself all appliances for meeting these demands. She alone has seen that if there is to be an infallible voice in the world, this voice must be a living one, as capable of speaking now as it ever was in the past; and that as the world's capacities for knowledge grow, the teacher must be always able to unfold to it a fuller teaching. The Catholic Church is the only historical religion that can conceivably thus adapt itself to the wants of the present day, without virtually ceasing to be itself. It is the only religion that can keep its identity without losing its life, and keep its life without losing its identity; that can enlarge its teachings without changing them; that can be always the same, and yet be always developing.

All this, of course, does not prove that Catholicism is the truth; but it will show the theist that, for all that the modern world can tell him, it may be. And thus much at least will by-and-by come to be recognised generally. Opinion, that has been clarified on so many subjects, cannot remain forever turbid here. A change must come, and a change can only be for the better. At present the so-called leaders of enlightened and liberal thought are in this matter, so far as fairness and insight go, on a level with the wives and mothers of our small provincial shopkeepers, or the beadle or churchwarden of a country parish. But prejudice, even when so virulent and so dogged as this, will lift and disappear some day like a London fog; and then the lineaments of the question will confront us clearly— the question: but who shall decide the answer?

What I have left to say bears solely upon this.

Is Life Worth Living? By William Hurrell Mallock

CHAPTER XIII

BELIEF AND WILL

'Abraham believed God, and it was counted to him for righteousness.'

Arguments are like the seed, or like the soul, as Paul conceived of it, which he compared to seed. They are not quickened unless they die. As long as they remain for us in the form of arguments they do no work. Their work begins only, after a time and in secret, when they have sunk down into the memory, and have been left to lie there; when the hostility and distrust they were regarded with dies away; when, unperceived, they melt into the mental system, and, becoming part of oneself, effect a turning round of the soul. This is true, at least, when the matters dealt with are such as have engaged us here. It may be true, too, of those who discern and urge the arguments, just as well as of those upon whom they urge them. But the immediate barrenness of much patient and careful reasoning should not make us think that it is lost labour. One way or other it will some day bear its fruit. Sometimes the intellect is the servant of the heart. At other times the heart must follow slowly upon the heels of the intellect.

And such is the case now. For centuries man's faith and all his loftier feelings had their way made plain before them. The whole empire of human thought belonged to them. But this old state of things endures no longer. Upon this Empire, as upon that of Rome, calamity has at last fallen. A horde of intellectual barbarians has burst in upon it, and has occupied by force the length and breadth of it. The result has been astounding. Had the invaders been barbarians only, they might have been repelled easily; but they were barbarians armed with the most powerful weapons of civilisation. They were a phenomenon new to history: they showed us real knowledge in the hands of real ignorance; and the work of the combination thus far has been ruin, not reorganisation. Few great movements at the beginning have been conscious of their own true tendency; but no great movement has mistaken it like modern Positivism. Seeing just too well to have the true instinct of blindness, and too ill to have the proper guidance from sight, it has tightened its clutch upon the world of thought, only to impart to it its own confusion. What lies before men now is to reduce this confusion to order, by a patient and calm employment of the intellect. Intellect itself will never re-kindle faith, or restore any of those powers that are at present so failing and so feeble; but it will work like a pioneer to prepare their way before them, if they are ever revived otherwise, encouraged in its labours, perhaps not even by hope, but at any rate by the hope of hope.

As a pioneer, and not as a preacher, I have tried to indicate the real position in which modern knowledge has placed us, and the way in which it puts the problem of life before us. I have tried to show that, whatever ultimately its tendency may prove to be, it cannot be the tendency that, by the school that has given it to us, it is supposed to have been; and that it either does a great deal more than that school thinks it does, or a great deal less. History would teach us this, even if nothing else did. The school in question has proceeded from denial to denial, thinking at each successive moment that it had reached its final halting-place, and had struck at last on a solid and firm foundation. First, it denied the Church to assert the Bible; then it denied the Bible to assert God; then it denied God to assert the moral dignity of man: and there, if it could remain, it would. But what it would do is of no avail. It is not its own master; it is compelled to move onwards; and now, under the force of its own relentless logic, this last resting-place is beginning to fail also. It professed to compensate for its denials of God's existence by a freer and more convincing re-assertion of man's dignity. But the principles which obliged it to deny the first belief are found to be even more fatal to the substitute. 'Unless I have seen with my eyes I will not believe,' expresses a certain mental tendency that has always had existence. But till Science and its positive methods began to dawn on the world, this tendency was vague and wavering. Positive Science supplied it with solid nutriment. Its body grew denser; its shape more and more definite; and now the completed portent is spreading its denials through the whole universe. So far as spirit goes and spiritual aspirations, it has left existence empty, swept and garnished. If spirit is to enter in again and dwell there, we must seek by other methods for it. Modern thought has not created a new doubt; it has simply made perfect an old one; and has advanced it from the distant regions of theory into the very middle of our hearts and lives. It has made the question of belief or of unbelief the supreme practical question for us. It has forced us to stake everything on the cast of a single die. What are we? Have we been hitherto deceived in ourselves, or have we not? And is every hope that has hitherto nerved our lives, melting at last away from us, utterly and for ever? Or are we indeed what we have been taught to think we are? Have we indeed some aims that we may still call high and holy—still some aims that are more than transitory? And have we still some right to that reverence that we have learnt to cherish for ourselves?

Here lie the difficulties. The battle is to be fought here—here at the very threshold—at the entrance to the spiritual world. Are we moral and spiritual beings, or are we not? That is the decisive question, which we must say our Yes or No to. If, with our eyes open, and with all our hearts, it be given us to say Yes—to say Yes without fear, and firmly, and in the face of everything—then there will be little more to fear. We shall have fought the good fight, we shall have kept the faith; and whatever we lack more, will without doubt be added to us. From this belief in ourselves we shall pass to the belief in God, as its only rational basis and its only emotional completion; and, perhaps, from a belief in God, to a recognition of His audible voice amongst us. But at any rate, whatever after-difficulties beset us, they will not be new difficulties; only those we had braved at first, showing themselves more clearly.

But that first decision—how shall we make it? Who or what shall help us, or give us counsel? There is no evidence that can do so in the sensible world around us. The universe, as positive thought approaches it, is blind and dumb about it. Science and history are sullen, and blind, and dumb. They await upon our decision before they will utter a single word to us: and that decision, if we have a will at all, it lies with our own will—with our will alone, to make. It may, indeed, be said that the will has to create itself by an initial exercise of itself, in an assent to its own existence. If it can do this, one set of obstacles is surmounted; but others yet confront us. The world into which the moral will has borne itself—not a material world, but a spiritual—a world which the will's existence alone makes possible, this world is not silent, like the other, but it is torn and divided against itself, and is resonant with unending contradictions. Its first aspect is that of a place of torture, a hell of the intellect, in which reason is to be racked for ever by a tribe of sphinx-like monsters, themselves despairing. Good and evil inhabit there, confronting each other, for ever unreconciled: there is omnipotent power baffled, and omnipotent mercy unexercised. Is the will strong enough to hold on through this baffling and monstrous world, and not to shrink back and bid the vision vanish? Can we still resolve to say, 'I believe, although it is impossible'? Is the will to assert our own moral nature—our own birthright in eternity, strong enough to bear us on?

The trial is a hard one, and whilst we doubt and hesitate under it the universal silence of the vast physical world itself disheartens us. Who are we, in the midst of this unheeding universe, that we can claim for ourselves so supreme a heritage; that we can assert for ourselves other laws than those which seem to be all-pervading, and that we can dream of breaking through them into a something else beyond?

And yet it may be that faith will succeed and conquer sight—that the preciousness of the treasure we cling to will nerve us with enough strength to retain it. It may be that man, having seen the way that, unaided, he is forced to go, will change his attitude; that, finding only weakness in pride, he will seek for strength in humility, and will again learn to say, 'I believe, although I never can comprehend.' Once let him say this, his path will again grow clearer for him. Through confusion, and doubt, and darkness, the brightness of God's countenance will again be visible; and by-and-by again he may hear the Word calling him. From his first assent to his own moral nature he must rise to a theism, and he may rise to the recognition of a Church—to a visible embodiment of that moral nature of his, as directed and joined to its one aim and end—to its delight, and its desire, and its completion. Then he will see all that is high and holy taking a distinct and helping form for him. Grace and mercy will come to him through set and certain channels. His nature will be redeemed visibly from its weakness and from its littleness—redeemed, not in dreams or in fancy, but in fact. God Himself will be his brother and his father; he will be near akin to the Power that is always, and is everywhere. His love of virtue will be no longer a mere taste of his own: it will be the discernment and taking to himself of the eternal strength and of the eternal treasure; and, whatever he most reveres in mother, or wife, or sister—this he will know is holy, everywhere and for ever, and is exalted high over all things in one of like nature with theirs, the Mother of grace, the Parent of sweet clemency, who will protect him from the enemy, and save him in the hour of death.

Such is the conception of himself, and of his place in existence, that, always implicit in man, man has at last developed. He has at last conceived his race—the faithful of it—as the bride of God. Is this majestic conception a true one, or is it a dream only, with no abiding substance? Is it merely a misty vision rising up like an exhalation from the earth, or does a something more come down to it out of heaven, and strike into it substance and reality? This figure of human dreams has grown and grown in stature: does anything divine descend to it, and so much as touch its lips or its lifted hands? If so, it is but the work of a moment. The contact is complete. Life, and truth, and force, like an electric current, pass into the whole frame. It lives, it moves, it breathes: it has a body and a being: the divine and the eternal is indeed dwelling amongst us. And thus, though mature knowledge may seem, as it still widens, to deepen the night around us; though the universe yawn wider on all sides of us, in vaster depths, in more unfathomable, soulless gulfs; though the roar of the loom of time grow more audible and more deafening in our ears—yet through the night and through the darkness the divine light of our lives will only burn the clearer: and this speck of a world as it moves through the blank immensity will bear the light of all the worlds upon its bosom.

Thinkers like Mr. Leslie Stephen say that such beliefs as these belong to dreamland; and they are welcome if they please to keep their names. Their terminology at least has this merit, that it recognises the dualism of the two orders of things it deals with. Let them keep their names if they will; and in their language the case amounts to this—that it is only for the sake of the dreams that visit it that the world of reality has any certain value for us. Will not the dreams continue, when the reality has passed away?

www.ingramcontent.com/pod-product-compliance
Lightning Source LLC
Chambersburg PA
CBHW081618100526
44590CB00021B/3498